DOMESTIC BLISS

SIMPLE WAYS
TO ADD STYLE
TO YOUR LIFE

RITA KONIG

A Fireside Book
PUBLISHED BY SIMON & SCHUSTER
New York   London   Toronto   Sydney   Singapore

Fireside
Rockefeller Center
1230 Avenue of the Americas
New York, NY 10020

Text copyright © 2002 by Rita Konig
Illustrations copyright © 2002 by Sam Wilson

All rights reserved,
including the right of reproduction
in whole or in part in any form.

First Fireside Edition 2003

Originally published in 2002 in Great Britain by Ebury Press, Random House

Published by arrangement with Random House Publishing Group

FIRESIDE and colophon are registered trademarks
of Simon & Schuster, Inc.

For information regarding special discounts for bulk purchases,
please contact Simon & Schuster Special Sales at 1-800-456-6798
or business@simonandschuster.com

Designed by Julie Martin

Manufactured in China

10 9 8 7 6 5 4 3 2 1

Library of Congress Cataloging-in-Publication data is available.

ISBN 0-7432-5213-6

CONTENTS

INTRODUCTION

Most of us lead chaotic lives, with little time or space for luxury, or for fluffing around the house making it look fabulous. We need to learn how to gain the most benefit from the little free time we have—and that involves both really enjoying our relaxation time and making the best of life's chores. The home is at the center of our lives, and a harmonious home leads to a more blissful life.

I would never argue that vacuuming is a joy, or that woman was designed to cook. But I do think that we should force into submission the aspects of domesticity that cannot be avoided. A little prettiness in the linen closet lessens the dread of having to open that door . . . just as a delicious smell in the bathroom eases the shock of those early weekday starts.

Decorating is more about living than about pots of paint. Laying the table or making your bed can change the look of a room in a minute; preparing a tantalizing coffee tray after dinner is going to make a far greater impact on your guests than the trim on your curtains. I am not a great maker of things and would not consider for a second taking on any project requiring either a lot of preparation or Scotch tape and an old toilet paper roll, so there is no need to panic on that front. I can't cook either, but the simple truth is that, despite more TV cooking programs than ever, most of the rest of the country can't or won't either. I do not believe that the modern woman needs to know how to do everything herself; she just needs to know where to get it from.

It is important to come home at the end of the day to a house that smells good, is comfortable and suits the way you live. There is a lot of pleasure to be had in the small things; for example, spraying your sheets with linen spray makes getting into bed at the end of the day even more enjoyable than it is normally. Making sure you have enough cupboard space is important: it is so much easier to put clutter out of sight than to live surrounded by piles of things that you constantly move from one side of the room to the other until you end up throwing them out in despair.

Decorating can feel like a huge commitment—people fear living with the same thing for the rest of their lives. Of course, it is not possible to endlessly change the look of your home on a whim, but it is possible to alter the details regularly and, in this way, for mundane and everyday things to take on a more stylish role. We are perfectly able to get dressed in the morning and put together some sort of look—well, a room is no different. With decorating and styling one's life, as with any project, if you take each step at a time, rather than panicking too much about the whole picture, it will be a lot more fun and you might end up with something that looks good.

I hope that you don't find this book too bossy, I hope that it puts a smile on your face sometimes and I hope that it inspires you. There is never any real need to get in a panic over a pair of curtains or a dinner party—your home should simply be about having a good time, either on your own or surrounded by your friends, and that is really what *Domestic Bliss* is setting out to achieve.

Enjoy!

Love, Rita

PLAYING
HOSTESS

PLAYING HOSTESS

Inviting people to your home is really the very best thing. Whether they are dropping in for a drink or two or coming to stay for a long weekend or a week, there can be nothing better—except perhaps that feeling you get when you have entertained them so successfully that they are asking when they can come again before they have even left.

This chapter is about how to be around your friends in your home when you are entertaining, parts of which are really easy and parts of which are really hard. Among the latter, I would include coming out with your prerecorded "Oh, that old thing, don't even think about it, it couldn't matter less. Just let me clear away those shards of Murano glass so you don't cut yourself." This follows the smashing of your absolutely favorite piece of frightfully expensive glass by some clot in your house and you would secretly be delighted if she did cut herself on it. It is also about not panicking when the oven blows up and there are eighteen hungry faces looking at you and it is 10:30 at night.

It does leave you wondering why on earth you would ever want to put yourself through playing hostess. But you really do, because having your friends around your kitchen table is one of the best things in life. Try to remembe: they are not the enemy, they are your friends. By entertaining, you live in your house to the full. It creates an atmosphere the likes of which nothing else can, and it allows you to hang out with your friends in your own environment. Inviting people to eat at your table is the ultimate way to seal a friendship, as offering people food and drink when they come to your door is one of the most basic customs of hospitality. I don't offer every Jehovah's Witness and door-to-door salesman who rings my bell a glass of wine and a snack, but I do love the idea that my door is always open. If you follow this route you are rewarded in the end because somebody really interesting will cross your threshold that you would never normally have met, or two people may easily meet and fall in love in your house—and be engaged the following week! That happened here once after someone called and asked if he could bring a friend. Your guests won't always be fabulous, though—you will have to feed a few freeloaders before you find a cracker.

THE PERFECT HOSTESS (URRRRRRGH)

Okay, so she sounds like hell, but that is actually Margot from the *Good Neighbors*, who I love, but for her ridiculousness. She is not a perfect hostess because she is too filled with affectations through her own insecurities and so makes everyone around her feel on edge. To my mind, the perfect hostess makes everything seem like it is a total breeze (but does scream when she burns herself on the oven door), is delighted that the house is full of people, nothing is a bother, she remembers to have a laugh, remains your friend, doesn't turn into some extraordinary form of Stepford woman—and is quite laissez-faire about her guests. There are all sorts of different occasions for practicing one's hostessly duties. Here are my favorites.

Tuesday night dinner

Tuesday night is reason enough to have people over: there is nothing on TV, you are neither at the beginning of the week nor even in the middle. It is quite simply the dullest

TO MY MIND, THE PERFECT HOSTESS MAKES EVERYTHING SEEM LIKE IT IS A TOTAL BREEZE.

day. Ship in the entertainment, invite friends over and don't worry too much about how many you ask—people always flake out at the last minute.

For this sort of dinner I would probably invite one person who will set the date and from then on I will ricochet around town inviting anyone I fancy. I will also go through my e-mail list and have a good look for anyone I haven't seen for a while and would like to have over. Whacking out a few e-mails is fun, it ensures contact and means you don't have to have a conversation. Then on the Tuesday, you call the people that you mentioned it to to check they are coming. At this point I have to declare my trump card, which is that I have a wonderful Italian friend living in London who loves cooking decent pasta. I have been known to plant him in my kitchen with all the ingredients that he requested.

You can't be too haphazard without a backup

plan, but even if you don't have one specifically, it will always be fine as long as the people you invite are fun. So: pasta, salad, plenty of wine and some chocolate cake and coffee for pudding. When you overinvite you have to be prepared for some people to sit at the table and others to sit on the sofa. This works best when most people know each other. It is really scary going to a house when you don't recognize many people and you have to pluck up the courage to go and sit next to someone you don't really know. You also don't necessarily have the opportunity to go and sit next to someone you have never met before unless someone organizes it, or you are very forthcoming.

More organized or formal dinners

There are times when you do want to be more Duchess of Windsor in your approach to entertaining and less Château Chaos. I keep meaning to do this but never quite

get around to it. Don't ever be afraid of asking new people and keeping it to a number that fits around the table. When you want to do this, you just have to work out carefully who else you are going to ask.

I have found the most entertaining and successful groups are when you get a bunch of people where everyone knows someone but no one knows everyone; it keeps them on their toes and it is more interesting. But you can't just put totally random groups round a table and be surprised when you get hideous silences. It is also a lot of pressure to put yourself under: juggling people, conversation and food all at one time is quite something.

You will know you have got the mix right when any of your guests makes friends with another at your house. Never get jealous or annoyed—rejoice in your genius hostessing skills.

Weekend lunches

The luxury of lunches at the weekend is that they can go on for hours and hours, because you never have to be anywhere in the afternoon, or even the next day, the way you do when you are at dinner midweek. The thing that I love about these lunches are sofas and newspapers combined with a very good Bloody Mary—think about actually mixing Bloody Shames (no vodka!) and then adding the vodka to taste. Everyone can really hang out and relax, and it is the time that I find I do, too, much more than when I am panicking about getting dinner ready.

For lunch I think you can have things that are heavier to eat and so easier to prepare than at dinner. Shepherd's pie, lasagne or osso bucco are all delicious, but your heart sinks at the idea of eating this sort of thing at night (my heart sinks anytime I am expected to eat stew), which means that everyone is also more likely to get excited by the idea of dessert, too. Let the afternoon ramble on, and then you can either end up at the movies or go for a long walk.

I feel it is very important that walkers are met with a good tea when they get back. Inevitably they will have been rained on and are likely to return home soaked to the bone. So they want to walk in the house and be met with a very large teapot and hot buttered crumpets, which means that somebody has to forfeit the walk to provide this essential end-of-the-day ritual. I usually find myself sacrificing the walk to do this. It is hard at first, but as the first drops of rain start beating against the window, I generally get over it. It is worth remembering just how good it is walking back into the house for tea in order to get you out of the house and on that walk in the first place. I hate the idea of going for a walk until I am on one, and then it is lovely—as long as it is on the flat it is the perfect time to catch up on the gossip with a friend, uninterrupted by the whining of a mobile telephone or the chattering of a small child.

Sometimes it is a good idea just to take some time out. Get into the kitchen and start doing something therapeutic, like the dishes.

The perfect week

SUNDAY Cinema or cozy plate of spaghetti with a friend. Some people hate doing things on a Sunday night and like to stay home and psych themselves up for the week. Personally, I still have a going-back-to-school hangover about Sunday nights and can't understand why you would want to add to the horror of it by doing that.

MONDAY TV supper. This can either be alone or with someone else. If you are alone, this is made a lot better by preparing something delicious for yourself. I find it very easy to slump on the sofa and not move again until I crawl into bed (very unsatisfactory). If you get something delicious for supper, you suddenly find you have a structure to your evening. Come home, have a lovely hot bath, get into your nightie, light some scented candles and a fire (if you have one), work out what the television has in store for you (which will be depressing, so get a video), cook your dinner and these evenings become a joy rather than totally scary—which is how I always viewed them before.

TUESDAY Definitely time to get some people over. Tuesday is really the dreariest of nights. Why is it that anything you might like to watch on TV is always on a good

going-out night? Wednesday, Thursday, Friday is when they broadcast all their best shows. Don't they know this is when there is other stuff going on and we don't have to rely on the television for entertainment? Keep this easy, just a couple of friends (see page 11).

WEDNESDAY If you are a half-full (as opposed to half-empty) sort of person, this is definitely the eve of the weekend. It is when people start to get out of their batten-down-the-hatches mode and poke their noses out for some action. This is an excellent night to entertain. Whereas on a Tuesday night you would probably want to keep it slightly lower key, on a Wednesday you can be slightly more relaxed about numbers and have more people. If you invite people on this night, you will find they think of it much more as a dinner party than coming around for supper.

THURSDAY This is the night to have a party if you are thinking of having one. People are pretty relaxed about staying up late and still being able to scrape themselves through Friday in the office. It is better than a Friday because you lose quite a few who might be going away for the weekend.

FRIDAY Friday night is most definitely the going-out night. Don't do anything at home, get your glad rags on, go and celebrate the end of the week with a couple of martinis in a glamorous hotel bar with friends, and see what happens.

SATURDAY Well, you want to be out this night, so give yourself a rest! But Saturday lunch is a real treat as you can spend all afternoon sitting around gossiping with a girlfriend or boyfriend. Saturday lunch does not have the group mentality that a Sunday lunch has, although lunch parties are lovely on a Saturday as they seem to make the weekend last longer.

SUNDAY Sunday lunch with a whole pile of friends, newspapers and Bloody Marys has got to be the best thing ever, hasn't it?

HAVING THE HOSTESS BLUES

There are three moments when you get the hostess blues: before, during or after a dinner, lunch or party. Generally, I get them after a party and before a dinner. The predinner ones aren't so much blues as chucking pans at the wall in fury. I have begun to realize that people are extraordinarily unreliable. I have often joked that one should always overinvite so you are left with the right number of people once half of them have blown you off and that you should never go to buy the food until 7 P.M. To call at 7 P.M. to decline an invitation is just laziness on the part of the guest, and I am now issuing cancellation times with my invitations: please blow off before 11 A.M. on the day you are expected. I also have a list on the fridge of those people who have canceled on me at the last minute and why. Obviously, this happens only among a rather spoiled group who have far too many lovely things to do. For most people, it is a treat to be invited to eat at a friend's house, and as a hostess it is important to create an air of excitement around your invitations to prevent this from happening.

Declaring disasters

When it all goes wrong in the middle of a dinner party, DO NOT cry. I do believe in declaring disasters but always with a smile. I had some people to dinner in the summer and I was at a loss for what to cook. Frankly, I was getting sick of roast chicken and I don't know how to cook anything else. So, while I was having a nervous breakdown in the middle of the largest supermarket in London (where I couldn't find anything), I had this brainstorm. I would just make a delicious huge salad. Perfect—at least until my friend Toby (who has an awful lot in common with Homer Simpson when it comes to both food and morals) arrived, looked at it and asked where dinner was. I told him that was it. "But where is the meat?" "In the salad," I told him. "And what about the potatoes?" "They are in there, Toby."

A much nicer friend, Abe, saved the evening by going out to get a pizza once the salad had been inhaled and there were still a lot of hungry faces around the table. But the weird thing about people, particularly the English, is that they love disasters. I think that is why we are really so good at home during a war. Bunker spirit and all that is something that we do well, so try your best not to worry when it all goes slightly off track. But it is imperative that you do do something about it, as it is only a real disaster when you think that if you ignore the problem, no one else will notice it either.

Sometimes it is a good idea just to take some time out. Get into the kitchen and start doing something therapeutic, like the dishes. I often find myself doing this at dinners (only my own), sometimes because there are no more chairs around the table, but often because I find that I cannot cope with the level of noise any longer and am just in need of a breather.

If you do this, you sometimes find that somebody will follow you, someone who may also need time out. It is really the perfect thing, as you have a chance to chat one-

THERE ARE THREE MOMENTS WHEN YOU GET THE HOSTESS BLUES: BEFORE, DURING OR AFTER A DINNER, LUNCH OR PARTY.

on-one with one of your friends and prepare the next course quite calmly. If you are about to go on to coffee, having a chat in the kitchen first enables you to be completely relaxed in the way you deal with those people who would like to go back to sitting on a sofa and to leave those who would like to stay sitting in the dining room. You don't have to suddenly stand up and tell everyone to move. I really disapprove of this, and such behavior gives me mid-party crisis as a guest; too much ordering around just isn't very relaxing. Of course it comes like a gift from God when you are being stultified by some stiff, but generally I hate it.

And *never* take the women through and leave the men to drink port and smoke cigars in the dining room—it is pretentious and silly. The thing that I object to most about this is that if you are somewhere where this happens, the men inevitably are quite dull (otherwise they wouldn't be doing it) and so you go through and they talk utter arrogant nonsense, tilting back on their chairs and guffawing among a cloud of cigar smoke. The girls sit around and start having an uproarious time gossiping, and then the men come in and interrupt when they feel like it. Urrrgh—it makes me insane with irritation.

HAVING PEOPLE TO STAY

I still get rather excited about waking up in the morning and there being friends around. I know that it is quite childish, because it really is a hangover from whispering all night with a friend on a folding bed.

A beautiful guest bedroom and having friends popping in and out has got to be one of the great pleasures of life. There are things you can do for guests that would be impossible to maintain in your everyday life, which is why it's fun and not a drudge to do them. Those extra frivolities are what makes someone comfortable and feel welcome. It is extraordinary how different it feels arriving in a house where your host is ready for you and excited about your arrival compared with when there is a rather fraught atmosphere and your stay is obviously extremely inconvenient for everyone.

If you are having someone to stay for longer than a night, you may want to make sure they feel able to help themselves to whatever they need. You don't want to be asking constantly if they need a drink or something to eat, and it often makes it much easier to have someone around who is able to infiltrate themselves into your life. Show them where everything is and make it clear that you would like them to help themselves. You will probably find they will still need to be offered things, as people do find it quite hard to help themselves too much, unless they are very good friends. You may also need to get used to it yourself, as it can be a bit strange having someone too much at ease around your home, picking up the phone and piling into the wine cellar. By working out what you like and letting your guest know how everything works, you will find that things become a lot easier for both of you.

A beautiful guest bedroom and having friends popping in and out has got to be one of the great pleasures of life.

Fluffing up the bedroom

Naturally you need to give some thought as to what might suit the guest, male or female, old school or modern. The bed is the obvious place to start, and you can make it more comfortable with layers, folding wonderful old blankets across the end for the male guest, or antique Welsh ones for the stylish girl. Acres of white linen and broiderie anglaise are ideal for most mothers-in-law. Hot-water bottles in winter and delicious dressing gowns, hotel style, cost little extra effort. Electric blankets can be a bit of a dilemma; for some people the idea of a warm bed is about as appealing as a glass of lukewarm water, and it should not be used as an alternative to central heating.

There are key things in guest bedrooms that are often overlooked: enough pillows and a bedside light, for example. I know this sounds totally mad, but there have been many times when I have had to grope my way from the bedroom door to the bed, stubbing, of course, my toes along the way. This does not fit very well with the joy of switching out the lights as you are unable to hold your eyes open a second longer. Squishy pillows are essential; a single long pillow is by no means enough and is too much like boarding school or childhood. If you have any square pillows, these are the most comfortable. The bed has got to be deliciously cozy, and extra blankets on the end look pretty. They also mean that should your guests get cold in the night, they can pull them up. Everyone lives by such different temperatures; some live in very warm houses and others like a slight chill, so it is a good idea to offer the extra blankets.

The more luxurious you make the guest bedroom, the greater the amount of time your guests will want to spend in it. This is not meant in an unfriendly way, but if

THE BED HAS GOT TO BE DELICIOUSLY COZY, AND EXTRA BLANKETS ON THE END LOOK PRETTY. THEY ALSO MEAN THAT SHOULD YOUR GUESTS GET COLD IN THE NIGHT, THEY CAN PULL THEM UP.

by any chance you are able to find a television from somewhere to have in there together with some lovely books, it is going to be a place where your guests would probably like to retreat to in the afternoon for a siesta. Now, this might suit you very well, especially if they are staying for a while. I love staying with friends when there is an atmosphere of being able to run on your own schedule to a certain extent. It takes that pressure off both parties to have to entertain one another all of the time. Not that I have ever stayed anywhere where there was a television in my room, and I hate going to bed in the afternoon. Ever since I have been old enough to say that I don't want to, I have taken great pleasure in not doing it.

Treats beside the bed

So set about making your guest bedroom really cozy and delicious. Try to think of all the things you would like to find when you are away from home. There is much to be said for the approach of a chocolate on the pillow, and while you may think this is just going a step too far, it is quite funny. If you can't quite get to grips with a Ferrero Rocher, break some squares off a bar: it would be as delicious and look great. It does not have to be fancy; in fact, quite often the less fancy it is, the better.

Bedside tables are a good place to start. Of course, the really old-fashioned thing is to put flowers beside your guest's bed. This is the loveliest of traditions and if you have flowers in your garden, this is obviously the best place to start. One of my favorite things is the single garden rose sitting in a glass vase, but don't be put off by the seasons: in the early winter you will probably find branches with berries on that will look glorious. Where you are unable to have summer flowers, whatever is around should be fine.

Think of leaving a small decanter of whiskey and a tin of good biscuits for your guest's midnight snacks, or a jug of water and a small bowl of some delicious fruit. Don't leave out anything too big, like apples or bananas, which have too much in the way of cores and skin, but figs or plums, apricots, grapes and peaches, depending on the season, are more like it. Customize the snack to each guest, and try to think of what you would really like to find in a bedroom when you are away, as that is usually a pretty sure way of getting it right.

Make the table fantastically luxurious, too. In old-fashioned houses you often find writing paper and envelopes, which are always rather tempting for sitting down and sending out gossipy letters in that Jane Austen fashion, but quite unrealistic. Postcards are much easier and more likely to get written; leave them by the bed with stamps on the back and a pen. If you can get to a post box, it is really worth knocking off the odd postcard while you are away, as they should not be kept exclusively for proper holidays. My friend Cathy is always sending me funny old-fashioned postcards from places she goes to in the countryside. They make such a delightfully welcome change from the usual brown envelopes and they are very good things to have around the house, perfect for kitchen walls or even just sliding behind the light switches and in the corners of frames.

Don't overlook books beside your guest's bed. I

step out of my front door with just about my entire life in my suitcases, but more often than not my book will still be sitting beside my bed. It is infuriating because it is just the best thing to do last thing at night. When you are staying with other people, your bedtime is slightly determined by theirs; it is not like being at home where you can pad around the house until you are ready to climb into bed and drift off. The thing that I have always found boring when staying with friends is starting a good book, which I then have to leave behind. I never remember to buy a copy once I'm back home, and taking it with me when I leave is a sure way of never getting asked back.

As a hostess, the best thing by your guest's bed is to have books of short stories or back issues of *Vanity Fair*. Keep a combination of subjects—old folklore is good (they feel like proper bedtime stories) as are short histories of the surrounding area. But for me a book of ghost stories is probably the best.

What to do if you don't have a plethora of bedrooms

Don't worry, you can still have people to stay, you just have to be a little more creative with the space you don't have. My best friend in the whole world, Honor, lives in Los Angeles, and she has an old French day bed in her sitting room, which I have slept on. In fact, once I slept there happily for two whole weeks. She does have a lot of space, as so many people in Los Angeles do in comparison to London, but she prefers to organize her space in this way, and in the daytime the day bed makes a really cool sofa with lots of cushions. Honor likes it because she thinks it is slightly Oriental in feel, and at night is the perfect bed. To live like this for any length of time you have got to be extremely tidy or else everyone goes insane with the mess. Unmade beds are bad enough in your bedroom, but in your sitting room they are totally intolerable.

The day bed option is very good for studies or a sound investment if you have a room that you want to double as something other than just a spare bedroom. I find that sofa beds are just the worst; they are uncomfortable sofas and uncomfortable beds, and should you ever want to sell one, you would probably find it difficult to just get someone to take it off your hands. So, what to do when you don't even have the extra room for a study-cum-spare bedroom or a French day bed? You can make the sofa in your sitting room as cozy as any bed. Make it as you would make a regular bed: take off the back cushions, if it has any, put a bottom sheet on the seat cushions, and then either a duvet or sheets and blanket on the top. Put the lovely things that you would put on a bedside table on the end table and make sure there is a lamp for your guest to read by. Suddenly you will rather regret that you aren't getting into it yourself. This sort of arrangement is only really good for the overnight guest, as you can't exist happily with someone living so on top of you, and there is nowhere for them to put their clothes and things.

If you know you are going to want to put up people on your sofa, there are measures you can take when decorating to make this tolerable. For example, for one of the end tables to your sofa you could have a small chest of drawers, which means that there is at least somewhere for the clothes to go. A burst suitcase in your sitting room for any longer than five minutes is just impossible.

Bathrooms for the guest

Like leaving my book at home, I can find myself without a

toothbrush really easily, or my tweezers, or just about any number of things that should be in my bulging toiletries bag. Putting together all the necessities in your bathroom is another styling opportunity not to be missed. You get a smug satisfaction from making sure your friend has everything they need, and it is particularly fabulous when the praise comes as they find the replacement bits and pieces. Think what a joy it is to go and stay somewhere where the bathroom is filled with delicious bath oils and scrubs that you don't have at home. Making sure your guests find a lot of things to do in the bathroom is also going to give you some time to put up your feet.

There are different degrees to how involved you are going to want to get with your credit card before the arrival of your guest, and it will depend on who it is. But the thing is that it does not have to cost a fortune. A lot of the stuff will be in the house already, and if you have a guest bathroom it is a good idea just to keep adding the occasional thing from time to time. This will spread the pennies. You can also put things in there

from your own bathroom before he or she arrives, and if he or she is going to be sharing with you, then just put together a bath package in the bedroom (see opposite). Do not feel that you have to have everything on the list; just pick the things that will suit the person staying. Some of the items come as standard and some are truly like the Ritz in their over-the-top nature. Be careful that your guest is not laden down with a ton of stuff on his or her way down the corridor.

To keep all these things in order, either in your guest bathroom or in the bedroom, use little glasses, tall glasses and dishes. Q-tips and razors fit in short glasses or old demitasse coffee cups. Tumblers are incredibly useful for makeup brushes, mascara and lipsticks; dishes take all the other, flatter, makeup. I love arriving in a house and having some time to nest, and this is made more possible when a few bits and pieces have been left for me to get on

The perfect bathroom package
- Fluffy white towel, as large as possible
- Smaller fluffy white towel for drying hair
- A dressing gown on the back of the door—perfect for having breakfast in.
- Loofah
- Bath essences and oils
- Scrubs
- Face masks—free sample packets are perfect
- Body lotion
- Toothbrush
- Toothpaste
- Razors
- Tweezers
- Votive candles
- Alka-Seltzer (depending on guest and proposed weekend)
- Shampoo
- Nail files
- Hair dryer

NB: Please make sure there is always a wastepaper basket in your guest's bathroom and in the bedroom.

with. It is a rare treat to have time to sit down at a dressing table to do one's face properly, so doing it when staying in someone's house in holiday mode feels very spoiling.

Guests arriving after long journeys

I have arrived in many Scottish houses late on a Friday night, missing dinner and not being offered anything to eat and starving until breakfast the next morning. This is not because my hosts were not the kindest, most generous of friends, but simply because they didn't think that we wouldn't have eaten that filth on the plane. Tray dinners by the fire are really divine; there is something just magical about having something delicious brought to you in the sitting room. I don't really like being shoveled immediately to a room and offered a bath and time to unpack. I like to be in the thick of it, chatting and hearing the news of the friends I am visiting. It is a really good idea to have the tray dinner ready, so that it is not a big deal to sort out when your guests arrive.

Things being prepared for your arrival just makes you instantly feel at ease and as though this moment has been looked forward to. There is something really magical about arriving somewhere late at night—you are tired and slightly disorientated, excited to be with your friends and full of anticipation for the forthcoming days of fun.

Some people do like to go and get settled before they come down to join you. If you know your guest well and are aware of this characteristic, finding a steaming scented bath with fluffy white towels ready to get into is going to be beyond luxury. If I was that kind of person, then I can't imagine anything nicer. In fact, I do think it would be the best, particularly if you are staying with an old friend who can chat to you while you are in the bath and getting ready for some of that delicious bread and soup that is simmering away downstairs. These things are built on atmosphere—they are not going to cost any more than what you would have spent anyway. All it costs you is time and effort, which is what makes it so fabulous. Everyone needs to be spoiled, and spoiling the people who have traveled any distance to see you is wholly appropriate.

GOING TO STAY WITH OTHER PEOPLE

I get quite nervous about other people's houses and that is why I try to make sure no one feels that way when they are here. I panic about things such as the loo might not flush or what time should I wake up, or everyone will know each other and I won't and they will all think that I am a freak and not talk to me. Well, of course, it is never ever that bad and the loo usually does flush and I have never missed lunch or anything embarrassing like that and, if everyone is awful, which has never actually happened in entirety either, you can always observe them and make mental notes. Once you do that, ghastly people become rather entertaining. I am now often more excited about bumping into the really grim people that I have come across in other people's houses than the nice ones.

I once sat down with a duchess, who will remain countyless. She had a Labrador slobbering all over her and she talked at length about her horses. I was not really able

EVERYONE NEEDS TO BE SPOILED, AND SPOILING THE PEOPLE WHO HAVE TRAVELED ANY DISTANCE TO SEE YOU IS WHOLLY APPROPRIATE.

to enjoy the slobbering Labrador (I might have been wincing, actually), or the idea of riding very much, which absolutely horrified her, and she shrieked, "Oh Rita, you are sooooooooooooooo pavement." At this moment she shot up in my estimation, but I am not sure if that was the response she was looking for. I think that she was probably trying to intimidate me or get a laugh off everyone else at my expense (which she was welcome to). But whatever is was, it didn't work, as I let her know in no uncertain terms that she was absolutely right and that instead of going out marching across the moors in the morning I would be going shopping. That reined her in and I had so much fun with her from then on, playing up to her towny expectations of me over the rest of the weekend.

As a guest, there are also unspoken rules that should apply. I firmly believe that if you break something, it simply must be replaced, and this counts for the water tumbler as much as the piece of furniture. I find it so depressing when possessions of mine are broken by careless friends who appear to think it doesn't matter, and I am also horrified when I break something in someone else's house. (This is the moment, friends, to call and claim damages!) Broken things must be replaced or restored. That said, my tolerance level for carelessness around my home is diminishing and I am fast learning the cost of friends. You really cannot have blanket rules because sometimes a guest will break something and be mortified by it. You may know he or she is totally skint and that you actually don't really care about the thing that was damaged or can easily replace it yourself. But equally this doesn't mean that just because someone has less money than you, they have carte blanche to destroy your home without receiving an invoice. You just have to weigh it up.

Just trying to help . . . (PLEASE DON'T!)

Now this is a line that usually comes out of someone's mouth just as disaster has struck; it has often come out of mine just as I have really bossily rearranged something that has already been arranged. Being a helpful guest is a tricky path: when are you getting under your friend's feet and when are you really being a help? Well, I think the first thing to do is to chill out. One is only ever getting it wrong when one is eager to please and slightly nervous. When you are in your own home you are usually in some sort of control as to when to get food on the table or generally domesticating, even if it looks like a poor impression of the contestants on a silly game show. But it is great not to feel as though you have been abandoned in the kitchen and are nothing more than a slave to your friends. As a guest, general morale boosting is good. So sit and chat while your host/hostess cooks and then you can offer to peel or scrub while you are sitting there. Sitting is especially good, as you are not in danger of getting in the way—it is also always preferable to standing.

Another good tip is when the plates are being cleared and you (and half a dozen others) stand up to help, and your hostess says, "Please stay sitting," for God's sake sit back down again. It is my idea of a nightmare when everyone leaves the table, as it is sometimes easier to clear up by yourself and it can be very disjointing to the conversation when lots of people are bobbing up and down. There is nothing that will sink a hostess's heart faster than awkward silences.

You know what the other thing is, and I must admit that I don't suffer from this: a lot of women are very territorial about their kitchens. Actually, I lie, I never realized it until I just wrote that just now: I am. I hate people in my kitchen without me. It makes me very nervous, and I hate people offering to help with the dishes in the middle of an evening. You cannot believe how many people say, "Oh, come on, I'll help you do the dishes," and there are still people sitting at dinner. In fact, you are probably having a pretty good time with someone. The thing is, they have decided to go home, so have stood up to leave, announcing it very loudly (another thing I hate). But they then have a momentary feeling of guilt about the mess and so start trying to clear the table and get you into the kitchen. Are they nuts? I really had to insist against it once. I mean they were about to destroy my evening. Just because they want to go home they try to wreck everyone else's evening by clearing people's plates from underneath them and dragging you away to the kitchen sink, leaving the rest of your friends to think that it must be time to go home too. All because they are trying to help. Well, don't, or you will come back in your next life as one of those small insects that only live for a day.

. . . SIT AND CHAT WHILE YOUR HOST/HOSTESS COOKS AND THEN YOU CAN OFFER TO PEEL OR SCRUB WHILE YOU ARE SITTING THERE.

AFTER-
DINNER
TREATS

AFTER-DINNER TREATS

Maybe it's because I am extremely greedy or that the sweetest thing about me is my tooth, but I really love having something sweet at the end of dinner. I love it when there is something delicious brought with coffee; just when you think that it is all over, something more arrives. It really does matter how treats present themselves at the end of dinner. This does not mean that they always have to be smart, they just have to be thought about. There is a bakery opposite my old office that has all sorts of fabulous things; it is a treasure trove for the after-dinner treat. They have the most delicious macaroons that are just pure goo and come in chocolate, raspberry and coffee flavors. Their colors make them really pretty, and even more so when you mix together the three flavors.

AFTER-DINNER DRINKS
As I am basically a non-cook, the coffee tray is my chance to shine, because it all comes down to shopping and styling, and it works like a dream on your friends. I am sure that people get more excited about this than they do about you killing yourself to produce some fearfully complicated dinner. I find it is only possible to be good at something that you start off doing well. I mean how are you going to look forward to producing dinner if every

time you take your attempt at a double chocolate twice-baked and even more times failed soufflé out of the oven and it has sunk? The answer is, you can't possibly.

So start with something really simple. You will do it well and the more you do it, the more adventurous you get, until, before you know where you are, you have become rather brilliant at it. I have commandeered the really easy coffee tray, and sparkle every time people talk about my delicious coffee. It comes out of the same coffee pot as my friends have but I have hit upon a few tricks to improve on its flavor.

The most easily appealing thing to do is to serve coffee in glasses rather than coffee cups. I used to reserve the glass look for lattes only while I was trying to make them like they do in restaurants, where the milk and the coffee are separated. It is quite difficult to get stiff and frothy peaked milk out of a domestic cappuccino machine, and they are quite a commitment. However, it is really easy to buy either an electric miniwhisk for your hot milk or a thing called a creamer, which is a metal jug that you heat the milk in and it has a flat mesh whisk thing that you plunge up and down. Between that and the espresso maker, you've got a never-ending range of elaborate coffees you can make. Here are my favorites.

. . . start with something really simple. You will do it well and the more you do it, the more adventurous you get, until, before you know where you are, you have become rather brilliant at it.

Latte

This is phenomenally easy: simply froth up the milk, pour it into a tumbler (remembering to leave some space for the coffee) and then pour the espresso over the top. It will sink to the bottom, leaving a thick white line around the top of the glass. When you are serving these at night, keep them short, there is an awful lot of milk in them, which is difficult to cope with at the end of dinner.

99 latte

This is very silly, which of course makes it irresistible.
When I presented this to my friend Lucy during a particularly childish competition of who could make the most
ridiculous cup of coffee, she shrieked with excitement on
its presentation. It is a regular latte in a stemmed glass with
a Cadbury flake standing up in it.

Floating the cream

It seems to be extremely old-fashioned now to offer cream
with coffee. My mum used to do this when we were little,
but with everyone now about to have a heart attack if they
so much as look at a jug of heavy cream, it seems to have

disappeared from our coffee trays. What better reason to reintroduce it? My mum used to float the cream for us, which I used to love—you could get the cold cream on your lips just before the hot coffee. Sweeten your black coffee and then pour in the heavy cream over the back of a teaspoon and it will float on the top of your espresso.

Soy latte

Now, for the nondairy crowd—try not to let them get onto the subject, believe me, it is dull. Given half the chance, people so love to tell you about their dietary requirements and, even worse, try to convert you in the process. So stun them into silence with a soy latte. It should let them believe there is no need to convince you, as they will hopefully assume that you know all about the horrors of dairy already. A soy latte is made in exactly the same way as a regular one. Heat the soy milk and froth to your heart's content.

Cappuccino

Serving cappuccinos at the table is rather stylish. People love to watch things being prepared in front of them, and if you have your espresso pot and jug of frothed milk on the tray, it is easy. The fun part of making a cappuccino is the bits and pieces that go with it. If you go to a specialist chocolate shop or even a department store with a decent food section, you will be able to buy hunks of chocolate by weight. Look for quite bitter chocolate, like 67 percent cocoa, which is not too bitter but it is just enough so you don't devour it before you get as far as having anyone over. Put it on the tray with a nutmeg grater and rather than sprinkling cocoa on the tops of the cappuccinos, grate the chocolate. You can also put nutmeg on the tray if you prefer, or have both so guests can choose their own topping.

Sambucca

For some reason I have found myself with a bottle of sambucca in my kitchen. Such is my ridiculous weakness for a beautiful bottle that I bought some at the duty-free shop in the Milan airport while I had a few million lire (in the days of lire) weighing down my bursting purse. The label was fabulously old-fashioned, printed in lime green, black and red. I fell in love with it instantly, so I carted the bottle home and wondered who on earth was going to drink its contents, but then I discovered that sambucca is delicious in coffee. Indeed, I have one friend, Ruth, who asks for it every time she comes to dinner. What I really love is that she asks for that special coffee I do, which of course just makes me melt.

Serve the coffee in a tiny tumbler, as you would a liqueur, and then splash in the sambucca afterward. You could substitute the sambucca for anything and you could even leave the bottles on the table for people to help themselves, although I prefer my coffee to be served fait accompli. It is not that elegant to be wielding bottles of alcohol around. I know this probably sounds rather sexist and that in this world of equal opportunity a girl should really be able to help herself to alcohol, but I prefer to have it served for me. My dad used to put Tia Maria in his coffee, which my mother had a thing or two to say about, mostly it was one word that started with c and ended in n. I am not big on spirits and which ones are cool to put in your coffee and which ones aren't. So keep trying them until you find the one you like, and I would say the more common the better, Tia Maria is nothing on adding Kahlúa, which Lucy is quite partial to.

Vanilla extract

This is not only delicious but a good nonalcoholic extra for the drivers and AA crowd. It is good with espressos, cappas, lattes or macchiatos. It is somewhere short of the hideous syrups that are on offer in every coffee shop around town. You can either go into the baking section of

THE FUN PART OF MAKING A CAPPUCCINO IS THE BITS AND PIECES THAT GO WITH IT.

your cupboard and just add the extract to the coffee, or you can find some fancy bottle of vanilla in a gourmet deli. Alternatively, you can serve vanilla sugar alongside your regular coffee. Or if you are feeling really smug and ridiculous, heat the milk with a vanilla pod and serve the coffee with it sticking out, like a stick of celery in a Bloody Mary. I have not quite got around to doing that yet, but I am longing to.

Flavored coffee

I was first introduced to flavored coffee by my mum's friend Stephanie when I was quite young but old enough to drink coffee. Stephanie has always had the best new everything first. She was the first person to give me banoffee (banana toffee) pie and guacamole in about 1986 when they were new. Along with cream eggs and coconut, the flavored coffee was something that my mother always thought was disgusting—making it instantly intriguing. Stephanie would bring amaretto coffee back from America, which in itself was incredibly exciting, and now she has one called noisette crème, which I love and keep trying to get people to bring back for me from New York. One of the reasons noisette crème is so sought after is because it is reasonably hard to get hold of and so it is still a treat to have. This will always be the feather in your cap.

Most of the flavored coffees are pretty awful (the idea of raspberry coffee is filthy), but the smell of coffee and nuts is delicious. Be sure to draw the line between a good new thing and something that is new and horrible. There is nothing particularly extraordinary any longer about flavored coffee, but not many people serve it, possibly because the idea of it is quite disgusting. So the trick is to choose your flavorings carefully. You will be amazed

ALONG WITH CREAM EGGS AND COCONUT, THE FLAVORED COFFEE WAS SOMETHING THAT MY MOTHER ALWAYS THOUGHT WAS DISGUSTING—MAKING IT INSTANTLY INTRIGUING.

how much people love trying something new, particularly when they are expecting to be presented with a cafetière or an herbal tea bag.

Espressos and macchiatos

There will be people who prefer a short shot of caffeine after dinner, and while at first you will find these friends annoyingly dull because you will want to show off your skills with lattes and cappas, after a while you will find that you love them for being so easy. I do like serving espresso in a very small tumbler. In fact, those exact ones from the market that I couldn't think would ever be useful when I first bought them.

Make macchiatos in these small glasses, too, and make them like the latte so you have a very dark drink with a perfect band of white froth at the top. Add a lemon peel twist to the rim, like that fantastic gay assistant in the gallery did in *Beverly Hills Cop*.

If you have a little demitasse or two and would like to be able to show them off, it is lovely to give them to your guests with a piece of chocolate casually positioned on the saucer. For this, I prefer the look of a bit broken off from a bar (and it should be broken off at the corner rather than neatly in a square).

They still
have things in
France
in their most
ordinary
shops that
are
considered to
be rather
fancy in
England.
This makes
buying treats
there terribly
easy.

Herbal teas and infusions

You don't have to be restricted to coffee for total carried away-ness. Herbal tea bags have infiltrated even the most ordinary of roadside cafés, so you are no longer going to get anyone very excited by one of these. There is also that obsession with endless new flavors and blends; listening to the long list of what is on offer can be as tiresome as listening to Jeffrey, your waiter for the evening, reciting the specials he has for you. People are not very good at making decisions, and you don't want to break the conversation around the table with tea bag choices. Choose one or two that you would like to serve and offer those. Better still, make a pot of one and offer it at the table. I am quite difficult, I know, but I do hate being interrupted the whole time during a good conversation. Everyone drinking a different tea means that really unappealing problem of tea bags in dishes down the table, or worse, in the ashtrays, and they don't brew properly in a cup.

Rowan's (deeply affected) thé menthe maroc

Infuse a more than generous bundle of fresh mint (not spearmint or lemon mint) in a pot with boiling water and gunpowder tea (comes in tiny balls and expands into leaf). Add sugar—about 1½ teaspoons per person. Pour the tea into a small glass, pulling the teapot as far away from the glass as possible to make a long spout of water—so you look like a particularly pleased with himself Moroccan waiter (this oxygenates the tea). Then immediately pour the first cup back into the pot (harmless affectation— but it does stir it). Put a generous bundle of mint in each glass and serve. Do not serve this tea unless you have a good handful of mint, as a couple of desultory leaves floating like dead goldfish is known to be bad for morale.

Using flowers

You can buy camomile flowers and vervaine leaves in some health food shops and delis. The easiest place to find all of these things is in France, which is not terribly useful for one's weekly shop, but it is definitely a good thing to bring home if you are ever there. They still have things in France in their most ordinary shops that are considered to be rather fancy in England. This makes buying treats there terribly easy. I don't really understand why, when they are so close to us geographically, the fruit in their markets is just so much better. All those greengages, or *reine claudes* (such a good name), are soft and delicious. They hardly feature over here, so if you can bear to carry those home in your hand luggage, they are simply perfect to have with a little tisane at the end of dinner.

Canarino

This is Italian for hot water and lemon rind. I am sure you will agree that, like most things said in Italian versus English, it sounds so much better. What they do in restaurants is peel the rind off the lemon in one go so it sits like a lemon without a center at the bottom of your teacup. This is extremely good for you, and at the end of a heavy dinner it feels like it might do something about shifting all that fat you have just indulged in.

Ginger tea

This is just an all-round winner. It tastes good, it is extremely easy to make and it is good for you, as ginger is just excellent for your blood and circulation. There are people who swear it brings down fevers if drunk in quantity, so for a cold make it very strong and it should fight off those nasty germs quite quickly.

Slice some raw ginger and put it in a tea pot with boiling water. My godmother, Leila, who drinks this by the gallon, makes it with ground ginger (she even travels with a pot of it so she is always able to have it). Leila also maintains that she really is not into all the palaver of slicing up bits of ginger every time she wants to drink some. She recommends that for a cup you need a generous pinch of ground ginger and for a pot you need a couple of teaspoons, but it really depends on your own taste. You can mix it with a little lemon as well. Unlike many of the herbal teas, which, let's face it, smell delicious and taste of sweet absolutely nothing, ginger tea has lashings of flavor.

White coffee

The Lebanese serve orange blossom water and rose water with, or instead of, coffee. When it is alone with hot water it is called white coffee and is delicious. You can buy bottles of orange blossom water in any Lebanese deli. The bottles are rather beautiful and I would recommend having both orange blossom water and rose water on the tray with a teapot of boiling water. In this way, anyone who fancies it can also add some to his or her coffee. And people always rather enjoy doing these things themselves.

AFTER-DINNER CHOCS

Now, there is no need to panic when you are standing in the supermarket and there is a really sad collection of smart chocolates from which to choose. Do not go for substandard. While there are times when a Whitman Sampler is absolutely the thing, there are also times when it is better to look at the bars of chocolate for inspiration. There is nearly always a new bar of something on those bursting sweetie shelves that you haven't noticed before, and if there isn't,

look for the really old ones. Remember the old favorites from your childhood—your guests will gasp in admiration and childlike joy, much more than they will with the Bendicks' mint collection. Tunnoch's tea cakes and snowballs have been the most successful thing for me, as have Nestlé's new fudge bar covered in white chocolate.

The best thing about Tunnoch's is that they have not changed their packaging and so the wrappers remain a glorious silver and red foil. You will find that snowballs get quite a mixed reaction because, on the subject of desiccated coconut, the world is divided between those who like it and those who cannot stand it. These are both quite rich and so are good after a light dinner. They also only really work once and are best for their surprise element rather than their flavor, which in reality most people have grown out of, but your guests will all be tempted enough to try these blasts from the past. The little chocolate bars are easy to put on the tray because you can stand them up in a glass. They don't need to be very large like Mars Bars, because no one can eat that much, but remember to include them because it is just too dull when that after-dinner chocolate craving is not satisfied.

Smart chocolates are not by any means out of the question, but they are not necessarily to be kept for your smartest dinners, and the cheap chocolates are, equally, not necessarily exclusively for cozy suppers. There is nothing more spoiling than a box of Charbonnels being passed your way or a yard of Bendicts' Bittermints, which are the original and the best after-dinner mint. I just hate the mixed boxes, maybe because it makes me feel that I am going to get left with the mint crackle in milk chocolate. I am not only greedy but picky, too.

NONCHOCOLATE TREATS

Never think you have to do anything by the book, which does not mean toss this in the nearest fire, but it does mean you can do anything you like differently from anyone else. If you should feel like it, dump the after-dinner mints cliché without any qualms whatsoever. Those delightful little *reine claudes*, as I love to call them (I know extremely pretentiously), are just perfect during the right season. In winter, dates are good, too; not the ones that look like boiled cockroaches with the loose skins, but the sweet ones. Biscotti are also good. I am quite partial to the frightfully expensive deli-bought ones that have been dipped in bitter chocolate and can, in turn, be dipped in one of your glamorous cups of coffee.

Violet sugar

There are really two types of sugar to serve with coffee, the old-fashioned coffee sugar and La Perruche brown sugar lumps. I love these, naturally, because I adore the box and I think the brown sugar is rather beautiful in its random lumps. They look even better if you scatter some crystallized violets between them in the pot. I have always longed to find another good use for crystallized violets and here it is. I love it.

Vanilla sugar

This is a fun thing to serve with coffee. You can do one of two things: either buy it in a specialty food shop or put a vanilla pod in the sugar. You have to be careful of this, though, for every time I have seen it done, the bowl of sugar looks rather manky: the vanilla pod has got sugar stuck to it and there are old lumps of damp sugar and stuff in there too. Now I know that this has got more to do with the length of time it has all been sitting there, but the point of vanilla sugar is for it to be pretty and delicious and old-fashioned, so remember to keep it looking lovely.

THERE IS NOTHING MORE SPOILING THAN A BOX OF CHARBONNELS BEING PASSED YOUR WAY OR A YARD OF BENDICTS' BITTERMINTS, WHICH ARE THE ORIGINAL AND THE BEST AFTER-DINNER MINT.

PARTIES

PARTIES

Planning a party is almost the best part about it. Who is going to come, what you are going to wear, the drinks, the food, tra la la . . . endless lists, invitations, etc. That is why it is good to plan it with a girlfriend, as two heads are definitely better than one to bounce ideas off (not to mention two bank accounts). It also gives you more confidence, enabling you to ask people that you don't know all that well, and you will be asking people that your girlfriend doesn't know, which is always a good thing for broadening the gene pool.

THE EXCUSE

Where other girls might have biological clocks, I have a sort of party clock and it seems to go off every now and then. There just are times in the year when a party is necessary, and when that moment strikes, you have to do it immediately. It is best to decide and do on the same day. My friend Natasha and I decided over lunch one day in January to have a Valentine's party, and by the afternoon we had written all of the invitations, sprinkled metallic hearts in the envelopes and were ready to post them. The great thing about doing the invites quickly is that once they are in the post box you have set yourself the challenge and there is no going back.

The clock normally starts buzzing at dull times of the year, January is an obvious one, and Valentine's is waiting perfectly in February to be celebrated. The other perfect thing about Valentine's is that a lot of people hate it and long for a distraction. Natasha and I decided it was too hideous waiting for someone to ask us on a date; the only thing worse was actually sitting in a restaurant at one of the rows of tables for two on the said date. So we saved a lot of people that embarrassing cliché of an evening and a lot of others a night in thinking that the rest of the world was having a great time by holding a cocktail party.

The best reason to give a party is for the hell of it. Go for the drab months in the year because that is when people are the most up for it. If you feel you would like to have some sort of celebration to attach to your party, then look in the diary from the day you decide to give your party and find something that warrants it. My most recent find is the first day of autumn, which is a pretty good thing to celebrate. Some people get quite funny during the changes of the seasons, so they need to be cheered up or at least warned that it is time to start being weird. By celebrating off-season and giving your parties during the boring months, you will certainly get the most out of your guests because they will leap at the chance to get dressed up and shake their tooshes.

I have never been tempted to give a Christmas party, as the idea of being stuck at my own party while there are several others around town that everyone else is skitting in and out of rather panics me. There is also so much competition—people just compare your party to the next one and why would you want to put yourself through that? So give one when that spoiled group of revelers will thank you for it. I suppose that if everyone takes this advice we will be in trouble, but I think we are probably safe in the knowledge that there will always be people giving Christmas parties and if they aren't, then just adapt the thought. Christmas will obviously become one of those times, like February is now, and there will be three parties a night during March instead.

THE GREAT THING ABOUT DOING THE INVITES QUICKLY IS THAT ONCE THEY ARE IN THE POST BOX YOU HAVE SET YOURSELF THE CHALLENGE AND THERE IS NO GOING BACK.

> Remember to never complain about noisy neighbors. Just be grateful when they play ghastly music until 6 A.M.; it is called party credit.

The odd thing about dates is that they come around terribly quickly. I always find that with my birthday (July 29!—if I appear to be unbearably bossy, it's because I'm a Leo), one minute it's March and a ridiculous idea that July is anything more than a fantasy, and then it is the end of June and I want to invite far more people than I can fit. So I don't invite anyone and then suddenly it is July 25 and everyone appears to be on holiday and I still haven't invited a soul.

Birthdays are generally trickier than almost any other party, as they seem to carry so much baggage. First there is a lot of politics surrounding the guest list; people do tend to get offended if they consider themselves a close friend and aren't invited. The fact is that you don't always want the same people sitting around the table, which is important to remember when you find you haven't been invited somewhere that you think you ought to have. So, how to get around this tricky situation? Never apologize and never explain—it is as simple as that. If you don't apologize, it is a lot less weird, and for God's sake you will sound so silly if you try to explain. I must say I do find it extremely irritating when people assume they should be invited by me to things; it makes inviting them less fun, because it is no surprise and it is so appealing to have a party where people are as excited about coming as you are about inviting them.

THE CONSIDERATIONS

There are pretty valid reasons for and against having a party at home and these depend on several things: your attitude toward your home, how many people you want and how much you care about the general good relations maintained with the neighbors. All are overcome-able. Get over the new carpet, don't panic about the numbers and invite all the neighbors (they probably won't come and if they do it usually means they are rather good sorts). Remember never to complain about noisy neighbors. Just be grateful when they play ghastly music until 6 A.M.; it is called party credit.

My friend Damian offered to send his elderly neighbors to a groovy hotel while he and his eighteen-year-old cousins hosted a party (rave might be more accurate) to celebrate Halloween. I can't think of anything nicer, possibly because I know that none of my neighbors would ever offer it. But they were horrified; they felt that he was trying to throw them out of their home. Their reaction was one of being temporarily evicted, and they declined the offer and stayed behind to battle through the night, rather like the passengers who wouldn't leave the *Titanic*. Of course they had a miserable night and the police were called out several times. However, despite the stony ground his offer fell on I still think it is a thoughtful and pretty cool thing to do, but it would probably work better on someone younger. I would offer this only if you can afford to send your neighbors somewhere truly lovely; there is really no joy in being rehoused for the night in some shabby B&B.

As for the big carpet debate, when I look down at my beautiful aqua gray pure wool broadloom carpet lovingly cut and laid by Allan the carpet layer and I see the mojito speckles that sit all over it at one end of the room, they do remind me of one astonishingly good party. Even though I would rather they weren't there, I would have the party again. And hell, what would you rather, to have lived a little or still have an immaculate carpet? If it is the latter, please return my book to your local bookshop for a full refund immediately and read no further.

WHEN YOU ARE MAKING A LIST, PUT BOYS DOWN ONE SIDE AND GIRLS DOWN THE OTHER, AS THIS IS THE EASIEST WAY TO SEE HOW EVEN IT IS.

That said, the next time I throw a party I am planning on moving all the rugs around the room into temporary spots. In this way, when everyone has gone home and finished wrecking the place, I can move all my rugs back over the stained areas and be left with the beautiful protected areas. Despite having mojitos all over my sitting room carpet, I do still believe that put people in a beautiful environment and they will behave accordingly.

So, parties at home; do have them. What is the point of making your home lovely if you never entertain in it? People just love going to other people's houses. For a start it is much cozier than a public place—putting a whole load of names on the door of a bar is just simply a poor excuse for a party; it has taken minimal effort and therefore you get minimal effort out of your guests. Details are critical and every single one will be noticed and loved.

THE PEOPLE

Obviously the guests are the most important aspect of a party. Don't be scared of them. They are human, after all, and remember that they are your friends, which I have to admit is sometimes easy to forget, especially when you are watching them toss cosmopolitans all over your front room like a bunch of naughty teenagers. We all get so panicked by them, and I am sure that everyone is the same. My mum says that there are some people she is nervous about having over to dinner because she feels her house isn't grand enough. People pay her for her style advice and write about the fact that she has so much taste and is so clever, so you see it doesn't really matter who you are, everyone has insecure moments.

I was on holiday with my mother once, staying with quite grand friends of hers, and we were having a big dinner and inviting another two house parties to it. The hysteria going on about whether or not the table was smart enough and would so and so think that it was OK, blah, blah, blah, was amazing, especially as everyone had a great time. I think they were so relieved to be in a slightly more relaxed environment that all these super grandees relaxed and set about enjoying themselves.

When you are making a list, put boys down one side and girls down the other, as this is the easiest way to see how even the balance is. Don't panic when you have more boys than girls, or vice versa. It nearly always works out in the end; people always bring someone, people always drop out—it is pretty common to have 10 percent no-shows on the day of the party.

One of the best things about throwing a party is being able to invite the people you don't know terribly well. Never be nervous about this, and if you are, just put yourselves in their shoes. When was the last time someone new invited you to their house and you thought they were a freak for doing it? You didn't—you were deeply flattered, I bet. You need a good mix and you need also to be slightly aware of people knowing one another. For example, it is not possible to have a whole bunch of people who know each other intimately and then throw in the new person you met last week. The best groups are always the ones where everyone knows at least one other person but not every other guest. In this way you create a sort of social daisy-chain effect.

GETTING READY

It is not enough to move all the furniture and rugs out of the way; it is essential you make sure there are lots of places for people to sit. Set about creating lovely little corners, which are ideal areas for flirting and gossiping, with tables beside them for drinks and ashtrays. You cannot expect people not to spill their drinks if they have to put them on the floor, and it is the same with cigarette ash. And I am afraid that however much you hate smoking, you have to give in and go with the flow when you are hosting, otherwise all the most entertaining people will be huddled in the garden. It's as simple as that.

The flowers

Flowers are an especially lovely detail and quite important, although if you are on a tight budget they are the thing to cut back on. Go to the market on the day of your party and buy them cheaply and in bulk. Don't go for fancy arrangements with a bit of this and a bit of that. Instead, have huge vases of the same flower. A vase packed with daisies is a delight and there are also always little spaces for bud vases that just take one or two stems. This makes all the difference and you don't have to be Martha Stewart to make them look good. The bud vases don't cost very much to fill either, and they make a huge difference to the room. Go for bulk; there is nothing sadder than stingy-looking vases, and you need to get the scale right. Four sunflowers in a huge vase of water look wonderful and probably bet-

ter than a huge bunch. Only fill the vase one-third to one-half and make sure you keep the water clean. This applies to any of those large, tall-stemmed flowers whereas tulips, on the other hand, always need to be bought in bulk as one bunch is never enough, unless you are putting them in small vases.

It is a good idea to have a few small vases—pint glasses are useful and so are single tumblers. It is a good thing to remember if you are ever in an antique/junk shop and see a beautiful single glass that it can be used as a vase. Grouping small vases and glasses of different heights and shapes is really pretty. I found some great vases the other day while I was digging around a flea market. Two of them were old geometric ones from Murano and the other one was much dumpier and more rounded, I think probably English. They are all yellow and green and look great together. Don't feel you always have to keep to the same colors; usually it is best not to. There just needs to be a spirit that gives some continuity. Things in threes are good and according to the Chinese it is lucky to have things in odd numbers, which is a new thing for us because usually in the

IT IS A GOOD THING TO REMEMBER IF YOU ARE EVER IN AN ANTIQUE/JUNK SHOP AND SEE A BEAUTIFUL SINGLE GLASS THAT IT CAN BE USED AS A VASE.

West we want everything in pairs. There are so many cheap and good-looking vases on the market, so don't be taken in by the "good value" of a wide-necked large vase at a good price. Remember that you have got to fill it with something and you can all too easily spend plenty of money filling a vase.

THE BIG NIGHT

A really good tip I like is to get a few core friends to come early. It is dreadful being the first to arrive at a party and it is equally awful for you standing around the pretzels with the early guest that you don't really know all that well. It puts you off balance and it is to be avoided. Getting a couple of your best mates to come early means this never happens. They also calm your nerves and by the time the others start arriving, there is a bunch of people already drinking and chatting. The other solution to this is to arrive late at your own parties. In this way you never have to worry about that stagnant moment at the beginning and it is lovely to walk into a full room, particularly when they are all your friends and they are waiting for you.

The drink and the food

Try to do something a bit different. Everyone loves to be surprised. Cosmopolitans are beautiful because they are pink, but they therefore do have their drawbacks. Go for vodka-based drinks and you will rejoice every time you see one go over as you will know that your careless friends are actually cleaning your carpet. You need a lot of ice and, if you are having a lot of people, a barman. This may seem quite extravagant but it is a nightmare when everyone is in the kitchen helping themselves and even worse when you are spending the whole night acting as barmaid.

Your guests will always be as relaxed as you are, so explore the canapé scenario—they are just the business when it comes to easy food to serve. Forget the little smoked salmon rolls; everyone hates them and they are really dull, unless you are having a "nineties revival" as your theme. Instead, have sushi; you can go down to your local Japanese restaurant and get takeout—they are cold and easy to eat. Keep your eyes open throughout the year for other good things. Most foreign food is good for inspiration. Lebanese is delicious and so is Turkish. There are lots of finger foods, like stuffed grape leaves and chicken wings, which are great for cocktail parties. For our Valentine's party, Natasha cut about a thousand pieces of toast with a heart-shaped cutter for taramasalata. Toast is great because there are so many delicious things you can put on top. The heart toasts were as big a success as the ridiculously fancy sushi and dim sum that our friend Will Ricker produced from his restaurant E&O. You can also bake

new potatoes and serve them as canapés with some baked beans in the top or with sour cream and caviar.

Have little dishes of goodies on all the tables, because if you have got a lot of people in a small space it is such a bore having food passed around. I hate being interrupted every five minutes for an hors d'oeuvre that I don't want, and it is always just as someone is about to tell you some riveting piece of information. I hate to say it, but I am always delighted to see a sausage, just a regular, really delicious little British sausage with some mustard. Who said we don't have any idea about cuisine? There's also shrimp with cocktail sauce (not marie rose sauce, a mix of ketchup and salad cream you get in England, unless you are still on the revival night, but that delicious tomato and horseradish stuff), which I just love.

The music

The music is so important, it will make or kill your party. Everyone loves dancing, it is so good for you and how many times have you heard people complain about the music at a party, or say that it was brilliant because the music was good? After the war, when no one had any money but boy did they need some morale boosters, my grandparents (and I am sure loads of other people did the same thing) used to have regular parties at their house and everyone piled in and helped make a night of it. Some of the guests would bring food while others would bring some whiskey and then they just rolled back their carpet and danced all night while someone played the piano. Being sixty years ago, house prices weren't quite what they are now, so they did have a good-sized room to dance in, even if they had no cash, but the principle is worth following: when the chips are down, dance.

THE AFTER-PARTY BLUES

Now, these are very common and understandably so. For months you have plotted and planned, invited, arranged and gossiped and giggled. Then your friends have all arrived, partied, danced and laughed with you; it has been the most fabulous success and it is all over. The following day there is nothing to do and you have seen every single one of your friends the night before and they are all busy. You have not arranged anything because it didn't occur to you as you were far too preoccupied and you feel a bit like an overtired child. This is all avoidable—you just need to plan, making sure you have a postmortem dinner to pick over the party. You need only one friend and some leftovers for this. If there are no leftovers, then a very simple dinner will be fine, as one is usually feeling a little delicate by this stage. The postmortem is a really important part of the whole party process and it is not good to miss out on it. In fact, forgetting this ritual is probably reason enough to sink into a depression.

There is one other small thing that can bring a tear to your hungover eye the next morning and that is minor damage. I am afraid there is nothing for this other than a little anger management and a lot of stiff upper lip. You just have to get over it; the burn mark in the middle of the mantelpiece and the red wine on the carpet come with the party territory. Try not to find out who did it or it will color your view of them and it is really not worth it. Some things will improve with age and simply become reminders of a good night.

Important things for a good party (in order of importance)

- The music
- The people
- The drink
- The lighting
- The atmosphere. (This is usually created by you and the above; don't take the line "it's my party and I'll cry if I want to." You absolutely CANNOT.)
- Door policy. Don't have scary bouncers who are going to be rude to your friends. Whenever I have had a party where doormen have been necessary, we have told them to let everyone in and if they are not on the list, to ask them the names of the people giving the party so that at least you know they are not going to cause trouble.
- Don't panic about gatecrashers too much. Enter the party spirit and have fun and be pleased that other people want to come.

CAMPING AND PICNICS

CAMPING
AND PICNICS

Take the party outdoors and make it last over a couple of nights with a little light camping. It does not have to be hardcore and it certainly never has to be endured with picnic benches or orange tents. Surely it is about the romance of rustling leaves and fishing for your supper, and what you need to remember to take with you so that the fish actually tastes good.

Sleeping outside without a tent is the ultimate in camping. You run a bit of a risk, but if you want the outdoors, this is surely the best way to get it. Most of the times that I have slept outside have been without a tent, in the open air beside a fire on a fine night in summer. Take a bedroll with you and always remember your pillow. Beech trees are the best thing to sleep under as their foliage is too dense for anything to grow underneath them, so you will get the softest natural mattress. There is then the pleasure of waking up with the sun coming through the beech leaves, which is one of the most glorious things. But be prepared to be woken early. It can be 3 A.M., but this is part of the magic of camping and pixies and fairy circles and things, isn't it? You start living in a different time zone to everyone else. I have always found something quite exciting about being up before the rest of the country.

If you are not entirely sure that camping with no cover is sensible, then you can find a compromise between tented and open-air camping with a bivouac, or if you can get your hands on an old army surplus *Swallows and Ama-*

zons–style tent, then that is lovely. It is just that the modern tent is really the housing equivalent to a windbreaker, and how compatible are nylon and nature in the ideal beautiful world? Not very, I say. It is all about the campfire, the rustling of leaves and the telling of ghost stories with your dog lying close by, gently growling.

CAMPER VANS AND FILLING THEM UP

Of course, the thing we dream of, or at least what I would dream of, is an old trailer or the original VW camper van. These are styles that are much more glamorous and easy to make cool. I once spent one of the best weekends ever in a camper van. You get a sense of total freedom, almost from the moment you set off in one. All the wrong things happened to us, like we set off up the wrong motorway and didn't realize until we had come to the end of the pier at Southend-on-Sea, and then promptly broke down almost as soon as we got ourselves onto the right motorway. We then spent the night in a pullout and woke up beside a civil engineering plant, not the beautiful Suffolk beach that we had been planning on. But it didn't matter, we had filled our temporary accommodation with more comforts than home.

We had linen sheets with blankets and eiderdowns, a fridge full of delicious things for breakfast, lunch and dinner, and even cocktails. We had more electrical equipment than the local showroom, mobile phones, music, cameras and a camcorder. This was the ultimate "playing house" and I firmly believe that for all the people who laughed at us for not having sleeping bags and all those sorts of regular camping things, we had a better time for it. It is absolute nonsense that you have to be uncomfortable as soon as you leave your home, that you immediately re-

SLEEPING OUTSIDE WITHOUT A TENT IS THE ULTIMATE IN CAMPING.

place cotton with nylon. Why do this? I have never understood it. People think I am ridiculous, but I don't really understand why. I don't have a sleeping bag, so it makes perfect sense to remove the bedding from my bed rather than go and spend money on something as horrible as a nylon wraparound duvet, which is basically what a sleeping bag is. It also adds a whole new dimension to the experience if you get excited about your surroundings.

My good friend and stepcousin, Willy, is one of the chief people who thinks it is completely silly to fuss about whether things are pretty or not. He goes camping with a carton of cigarettes, which would just make me cry it is so Spartan. Lucy, on the other hand, has got camping and picnicking tapped. She collects camping gear and takes huge rugs (not travel rugs, Persian rugs!). And for the entire camping trip she will be building the campsite because, of course, that is the fun of camping, making your new home beside nature. Once it is done, Lucy then cooks delicious things over the campfire; no campsite is complete without

CAMPING AND PICNICS

the sound of sizzling eggs and bacon. It seems that camping is always about nesting and eating and chatting around the campfire and once you have done that, it is time to go home. It does beg the question, is there more to life than nesting, eating and chatting?

Camping kit

- A bedroll including a ground cloth, blankets, sheets, pillows, and a thick foam mat like a yoga mat or an inflatable mattress.
- A sleeping bag if you must. Try to find one of the ones that is nylon on the outside and brushed cotton on the inside for extra coziness. They are very good for sleeping in a hammock.
- If not, a full set of linen sheets with blankets and eiderdown.
- A flashlight
- Spare batteries
- A box of matches
- Cooking utensils
- A good book
- A guitar
- Tablets for purifying water
- Smuggler fishing rod
- Swiss army knife or a Leatherman
- A compass and detailed topographic map

MOTOR HOMES

I have just spoken to an old friend and his new wife, Cathy, on the telephone. He is rather eccentric and therefore extremely funny. One of his new ideas for the winter is to get a motor home. While this probably sounds neither particularly eccentric nor funny, Cathy is horrified. I am not sure if it's just the idea of wintering in a motor home or that for a stylish girl a motor home (and he doesn't want a really cool old VW camper or old RV, he wants a brand-spanking-new top-of-the-line one) is not very stylish. However, everything has an opportunity for great style; you just have to get involved in whatever style that is, and I mean get involved. Don't try to fight against it by imposing your own style on top of it. Like all things you start fighting with, it will become a nightmare. Start thinking about *Carry On Camping*, think of those fabulous swing sofas with huge floral prints in most seventies' back gardens. Start going to as many yard sales as you can and you will find this is a great thing, because it is completely separate from how you would style either yourself or your home. Having something like a motor home is so much fun, simply because it is a chance to be somebody different for the time you are in it.

DINNERTIME IN THE WOODS

But back to the eating bit. For the perfect supper, you have got to be near a river and be cooking a freshly caught trout. Include in your packing a pepper mill and a lemon, a small jar of olive oil and a smuggler fishing rod. You can either cook your trout in tinfoil in the embers of your campfire or in a skillet if you have managed to get the tripod together. Keep your nostrils alert, as you never know

HAVING SOMETHING LIKE A MOTOR HOME IS SO MUCH FUN, SIMPLY BECAUSE IT IS A CHANCE TO BE SOMEBODY DIFFERENT FOR THE TIME YOU ARE IN IT.

when you might stumble across some wild garlic. You can't really miss it and it is delicious to cook with. I don't think there is anything wrong with taking a few more things like fresh herbs, salt and some salad. It really depends on how hearty you are and how far away from the camp your car is.

I have never walked with a tent on my back and can't really imagine it being anything other than very hard work and a total nightmare. I was taken to Irian Jaya once by an old boyfriend of mine (funnily enough he became "old" on that trip) and we had to hike across these mountains (when asked what I wanted to do for our holiday all I said was "not walk up hills"!), then on through jungles. We carried backpacks and washed in rivers and slept in mud huts and stuff. It was pretty amazing, actually. What he thought he was doing, I don't know, but luckily we found some porters to carry our backpacks. Euan kept on carrying his to give his porter a break, but I couldn't make eye contact with mine for three days because I was so worried that I might have to carry it on top of the walking, which nearly killed me. I kept thinking of Julie Andrews fleeing over the Alps in *The Sound of Music* and trying to imagine that there were a gang of Nazis chasing us to spur me on.

All we got to eat were raw sweet potatoes and sometimes a pineapple. The pineapples were the best I have ever eaten; the minute one of the porters cut it with his machete (that was the other thing—all the locals carried machetes and wore penis gourds; they were quite a scary bunch of people), you could smell this delicious sweet pineapple smell. For the jungle I would recommend you take something with you so you don't get caught up eating raw sweet potatoes, which are just awful.

MAKE SURE YOU HAVE EITHER A "ONE I PREPARED EARLIER" TROUT OR A CAN OF BAKED BEANS HANDY JUST IN CASE THE FISHING IS NOT FRUITFUL.

But back to the more usual camping habitat of woodland with either a camper van or car. Don't hold back on any of the things that are going to make your breakfasts, lunches and dinners delicious. After all, when you are on a little camping trip, there is really nothing much to think about other than what to cook next, so you might as well make it really good. Frankly, it should really be just one long superdeluxe picnic. Make sure you have either have "one I prepared earlier" trout or a can of baked beans handy just in case the fishing is not fruitful. Purists would think this is a terrible thing to do, as it is part of the whole "hunter-gatherer living with nature experience" to go hungry if you have not caught your dinner. But, well . . . you could do that if you wanted.

Good camping food for the no-nonsense camper
- Baked beans
- Sausages
- Eggs
- Baked potatoes
- Tea/coffee

Good camping food for the all-style camper

- A Stilton
- Full English breakfast
- Some fresh herbs
- A pepper mill
- Olive oil
- A lemon
- A backup fish
- Some ready-made meals
- Real coffee

Good camping cooking gear

- A gypsy tripod—this means that you can hang all the pots and pans over the campfire instead of burning everything in the campfire.
- A grille for cooking on
- A kettle
- Pots and pans that can be hung from the tripod
- Coffee pot

How to build a campfire

Everyone has a theory about making a campfire. It is one of those things, like a barbeque and the TV remote control, that boys seem to feel they were born to. This, of course, is fabulous, but it is definitely worth knowing how to do it just in case you ever find yourself on a camping hen party or something.

Whatever the shape of the campfire, you will need to dig a shallow pit first and fill it with dry leaves, bark and small twigs. Dry fir cones are supposed to be the best and you should collect them while on country walks in preparation for camping trips. My lovely friend Daffyd, who is a Welsh hill farmer, recommends these very highly for the resin they have in them, which helps tremendously with the ignition of your fire.

When it comes to the shape of your campfire, there seem to be two very clear camps in which you sit: one is the Indians' and the other is the cowboys'. The tepee method is the most common for the modern campfire, for which you need to use young branches broken into lengths of about 8 to 13 inches. Arrange them like an Indian tepee and then light the kindling inside. Once the sticks have caught fire, start adding larger pieces of wood. It is important to build your fire gradually and don't pack it too tightly because it needs oxygen.

For the log cabin method (named after the old-style frontier houses of rural America by my good friend, but no relation, Willy K), you build a log cabin with branches until it is about 8 inches high. Then cover the top with more branches, light the kindling inside your log cabin and once the branches have caught fire, start adding larger and larger pieces of wood. Alternatively, take a bundle of fire lighters and a blowtorch, which should do the trick without too much effort.

HOW TO CAMP INDOORS

There are times when it is necessary to camp indoors. The most usual is when you have just moved into a new place and everything is still in boxes, the contractors are about to arrive and you have decided to live through the work with them. Although this is best avoided if at all possible, loads of people do it—usually because there is not much of an alternative. I did this a lot as a child, as we were always moving, rather like fully double-tassel tie-backed gypsies but without the colorful caravans. To the horror of our neighbors, we once spent a whole winter walking along a balcony in bath towels because the only working bathroom was in the flat next door. The fridge was in the sitting room and there was a toilet installed in the hall of one of the flats, which was moved only when a magazine called my mum to say they would be coming in a month to photograph her new home. It is hard to remain sane during times like this. You are never really clean because of the dust, and your tolerance level, I reckon, can last about a month. However, I also believe that anything is possible as long as it has a visible deadline.

Camping at home happens to nearly all of us at some stage; it certainly does when you have just moved into a new home. The thing is that you have to try to hold on to some standards and areas of luxury, even if everything else looks like a pretty good impression of hell. If you have nothing else, at least make sure that your bed is comfortable and you have a bedside table, even if it is a box with a cloth over it. Be sure that your bathroom has good towels and plenty of things that will make you smell good in it, and there absolutely has got to be somewhere to sit. Your life will be intolerable if you don't do these things, even if all of the above is going on in one room. The thing is, when your life at home is chaos it will have a domino effect on all the other areas of your life, so it is very important to try to overcome it in at least one part of your abode. For me, the answer to most problems is a few sensory treats.

PICNICS

Winter
The seasons obviously make different demands and winter picnics are rare treats that require careful thought; not just

soup in a thermos but delicious sausages, spare ribs and bananas wrapped in foil with melted Milky Ways (very good insulation material). Barbeques are great in the winter, especially if they are on location and not in the backyard. It is strange, but a barbeque in the garden is just depressing any time other than midsummer, whereas cooking food outdoors during winter almost anywhere else is really great. Beaches in winter are just so fantastic: crashing waves, and boots, hats and scarves around a barbeque or campfire. You can get throwaway hibatchis and baby Weber grills for popping in the trunk.

Campfires in the cold are so romantic and why not have a fondue. I mean you have got to be really cold and about to go on some sort of walk in order to burn those calories and that fat. All you need is a bottle of kirsch, a loaf of bread and the fondue set your parents got as a wedding present (and would still pass for new except for the fantastic seventies saucepan that it comes with). What an easy picnic, and it is certainly going to keep the cold out. For campfires I have found it is good to put the fire in a big old enamel/metal bowl. In this way you can take the fire away with you and do not have to worry about the scorched earth or potential fire hazards.

When you are in foreign countries keep an eye out for interesting culinary items. I was in a toyshop in France and found mini–frying pans for children that were usable. I wish I'd bought them now because I would love to take them on a picnic and have everyone cook their own egg. People are always excited by cooking their own food in both restaurants and outdoors, which I have always found quite entertaining, as they are often those people who hate cooking at home—and I include myself in that category. Actually, I lie. I am beginning to learn how to cook and

ONCE YOU HAVE A FEW FRIENDS, A SENSE OF HUMOR COMBINED WITH ADVENTURE AND PLENTY OF SCENTED CANDLES, SOME FRESH LINEN AND A BAR OF GOOD SOAP YOU CAN GO ALMOST ANYWHERE.

keep hearing myself telling people how easy it is, like those ghastly smug people do when they have just produced one of those stripy four-cheese-and-spinach soufflés. I haven't got there yet but, I can assure you, you will hear about it when I do.

Picnicking on foot

Buy a mini-thermos flask, which is perfect for long walks. Let's face it, long walks need a perk, and a hot bullshot is as good a perk as any—particularly when you have got the rain beating against your face and probably down the back of your neck. If I lived in the country and was the sort of person who got excited about going for walks, I would have a closet with a lot of picnic paraphernalia in it. Like, wouldn't it be great to have a bunch of little fanny packs for picnics? You could fill them with the mini-thermos for one, put in an egg and bacon sandwich wrapped in foil to keep it warm, the compulsory treat and something for the pocket. This would generally be some sweets—avoid chocolate because it melts; hard sweets are good.

The other thing that I would really like to have in my picnic paraphernalia cupboard is a few Polaroid cameras with a supply of film. Walks and picnics are often some of the best times that you have with your friends and family. The simple combination of being outside with the people that you love, lying around at a picnic or walking through a beautiful place is the time to capture it on film. The fun of a Polaroid is the instant gratification. They are perfect to give to children, setting them a challenge like finding five extraordinary things on their walk. Walking with purpose is so much more fun than an aimless hike across the countryside and it is great for children as it encourages them to look around themselves, which we so often forget to do. It is amazing what you see when you stop for a moment and take a look. It is also fascinating to get a look at what they see.

I really love Polaroids and I own a very old Land camera which takes great pictures that I have all over my kitchen wall. Above my desk I have six pictures from a walk in Scotland with great friends of mine; I think it might be the start of a new wall of walks. It is so easy to take a load of pictures, which then take ages to get developed and even longer to get into photo albums. And quite honestly, the majority of the pictures arc bad and they become a bore, until they are in the books, where they are lovely. But the books become too much like a personal history and a history of times gone by. Get the photographs up around you, on the walls, stuck in the sides of picture frames and mirrors (also see ". . . How to Spoil Oneself" on page 94). In that way you don't have to sit down and open the books to look at them; you just take in your holidays and trips with friends by osmosis, which must be good for you.

Spring/summer

This is a really glorious time and in England it is often when we have our best weather, so get in among the bluebell woods and the daffs and celebrate the coming of summer. There are a few things that you can treat yourself with on a spring picnic, like gull's eggs, which are a seasonal treat. They really are a treat as they are expensive and not what I normally, or in fact ever, have on my picnics, but the idea sounds great.

Spring picnics are really dictated by where you are, and also the weather in spring is so temperamental that sometimes you have to adopt the winter regime and other times you can take on a summer one. It's a mystery how we ever manage to get out in the first place.

Spring arrives around Easter time and if you are near the coast, it is worth buying up masses of fish and lobster. Lobster and crab are fabulous delicacies that I completely love because they are either very expensive or very cheap, depending on where you are, just like mushrooms (but we have to wait for autumn for those).

I was on Orkney once waiting for a small boat to take me and my old boyfriend (that was another one of those trips) on to one of the outer islands. While we sat and waited, a fishing boat came in with the day's catch and they had loads of crab and whelks on board. I had never eaten a whelk before and I thought their shells were rather beautiful. So I bought three crabs and a whole pile of whelks. The crabs were the best ones I had ever eaten, but the whelks—well, they were quite disgusting. I didn't even get as far as putting one in my mouth, as pulling the whelk out of its shell was enough to make me scream and leap back five feet. They are disgusting rubbery things with nothing going for them at all.

High summer

For high summer, instead of lying on those woolly rugs that make you terribly hot and sticky, think of using some heavy old linen sheets, which are so much more glamorous and comfortable on the backs of your legs. And for the food, you just need acres and acres of delicious salads and bun fillings, along with some crab claws and cold bottles of wine, and more good treats. My only real criterion for a good picnic menu is that it should feel as though the choices are never ending and that the leftovers aren't being rolled out.

PICNICS FOR JOURNEYS

There are so many different potential picnic occasions when on the move, it is most important to approach each one individually. For example, there is the long haul flight; whether you turn left or right the food is pretty filthy and so a Care package is a necessity. Equally, long car journeys always need good picnics, as the food opportunities en route will probably not be good. There are few things more depressing than take-away sandwiches from a motorway service station, and eating is an excellent way to pass the time.

Long haul flights

There is a key thing to remember when you are packing a picnic for an airplane: don't take anything that requires a lot of cutting up. It is impossible because you have so little space and nothing very substantial to cut with, so either chop beforehand or take finger food. Cold roast chicken is one of my favorite things for planes, as first it is one of the best comfort foods and you really need a little comfort on a plane, and second it is delicious and good for you. Traveling really takes its toll on the body and you want to be careful of filling yourself up with unhealthy things, like that filth on the trolley second only to school food.

Take a little salad with you with some dressing in a jam jar. Pasta is very easy to digest and it is, in fact, highly recommended when you are jet-lagged, so cold pasta salad is good. Whatever you take should be cold from the outset as hot things will be disgusting by the time you get to eat them and they also smell. I am always desperate for some chocolate during a flight, but then I am usually desperate for chocolate or sweets just about every four hours, so I always take some with me. Of course, that may not be the same for everyone but it is worth remembering that it is very hard to get hold of at 30,000 feet.

The other thing about taking a picnic with you is that it takes time to eat. You will take far longer getting your picnic out and having it than you ever can with the tray they give you. It is also far more civilized and somehow that always makes me feel a bit safer on a plane, a place where I just never feel completely safe, so anything that takes my mind off listening to the engine or panicking every time the pilot comes over the loudspeaker is good. Don't you hate that? Frankly, I would just rather he kept on flying than bothering to tell us when the iceberg that sank the *Titanic* is on our right. It just makes me so nervous, I always think the worst and expect him to announce that we are going to have to take the crash position.

There is a little tip that I have discovered: when booking flights on the Internet they ask you if you have a food preference. Click on this option and you will find food groups that you never knew existed, like low cholesterol, high cholesterol, kosher, kosher with no carbs, kosher with low salt, Pacific rim, Oriental, Asian, Middle Eastern, Hindu, modern British; the list is quite extraordinary. Being unable to resist, I once chose Hindu, which people found strange but I have to say that I was rewarded for my lateral thinking. When was the last time anyone managed to foul up a curry? The whole point about curry is that it is supposed to disguise revolting food, so it seemed better to have this than some truly revolting chicken pasta bake that I was sure the rest of the plane would be eating, and I was right. My vegetable curry and rice was delicious (or as delicious as can be expected). I did get a little nervous when the scones and sandwiches came around. I'm not sure what a Hindu has for tea and thankfully I'm still not, as I managed to keep quite a low profile while my Hindu afternoon meal was being offered around the cabin.

Car journeys

Car journeys basically follow pretty much the same rules as airplanes, the only real differences being that you can stock up along the way and you can't leave all your unwanted junk in the back of the seat in front and not expect to find it when you next get in the car. There is a picture stamped in my mind about picnics and cars, which is of a retired couple traveling along the motorway at about 50

miles per hour with a thermos of tea and a Tupperware box of sandwiches. Trying to pour tea in a car is really hard and I don't recommend it.

If you take pride in your picnics, start by wrapping your sandwiches in waxed paper and tying with string. That fabulous crinkling sound as you unwrap them is just so much more exciting than horrid old plastic wrap. Cellophane is pretty too, but it is less common in kitchens. I have found it is good to avoid tomatoes in sandwiches because unless you remove all of the seeds and watery pulp, they do make the bread awfully soggy, which sends shivers down my back. Some raw carrots and dips are good too. I know that the urge really is to stock the car with sweets at the same time as filling up, but for the smug, hey, I'm looking after my body feeling, crunch your way through the hours with delicious vegetables instead.

Journey picnics are much better if they have been packed by someone else; it increases the lucky dip element, or what Americans call the surprise factor. It is also much more fun packing a picnic for someone else. I find that I am far more likely to get into putting in little pots of mustard and chutney if that is the case. Include all the things you long to get yourself when you unwrap your lunch and you are on the path to being championed the whole way to your friend's destination. Treats are crucial, as the whole point of a picnic is to find goodies that you weren't expecting, so a slice of cake and some chocolate must be in the bottom of the basket.

Packed lunches for school outings

Packed lunches at school were always really exciting, anything to escape the standard issue mince with hairs it in or hot tinned tomatoes. And that anticipation all through the morning until lunchtime—wasn't there always one exciting

IF YOU TAKE PRIDE IN YOUR PICNICS, START BY WRAPPING YOUR SANDWICHES IN WAXED PAPER AND TYING WITH STRING.

thing in your lunch, or more to the point, someone else's? I have always found other people's packed lunches much more exciting than my own, purely for novelty value.

Make sure your kids don't compare and despair the next time they are at the natural history museum with their *Jurassic Park* lunch box. Unless you have one of those children who knows what he likes and cannot see any point in trying anything new, put delicious new treats in there all the time. Remember that fun-size packs of anything are never quite fun enough, so it is very important to add quite a few packs if you are keen for your children not to feed their therapists with stories of cruelty by way of near starvation. I do agree with children, though, when cruelty is seen in a parent who opts for the healthy organic packed lunch. Obviously if your children have packed lunches every day, you can't possibly feed them junk just to keep the best-mum-of-the-class crown on your head. But when they have packed lunches for school trips, it is very important to compete for the crown. E's are good.

JOURNEY PICNICS ARE MUCH BETTER IF THEY HAVE BEEN PACKED BY SOMEONE ELSE; IT INCREASES THE LUCKY DIP ELEMENT.

ME, ME, ME, ME
AND HOW TO
SPOIL ONESELF

ME, ME, ME, ME AND HOW TO SPOIL ONESELF

Life should be a succession of little treats. People talk about having standards and this is surely what they mean: making sure there is always something delicious in the cupboard for those nights in when you are exhausted from a long week. What else is there that restores morale more than an easy little pick-me-up? It is usually the small things in life that make you feel better. If stress is the second largest cause of heart disease, then this has got to be good for your health.

SCENTING THE HOME

We have all become quite accustomed to this: just about everyone has now brought out some form of room fragrance and every gift shop in the country is selling smelly candles (some smellier than others, so watch out; there is nothing worse than a cloying sweet smell in the house). However, I am not all that keen on the idea of spraying away the smell of cigarette smoke and cooking smells either, as that notion of putting one smell on top of another really bothers me. It is a little too eighteenth-century, when they just squirted a little more cologne on their wigs instead of having a bath.

The ultimate joy is to walk through your front door and be met with the cozy smell of home. People always remark on walking into a house that smells good and often it is dinner and there is nothing more welcoming than the smell of a good roast wafting from your kitchen. However, if you live alone it is impossible to organize this for yourself when you get home, just as it is to light a candle before you walk through the door, so pay heed to these helpful hints.

For entrance halls a bowl of potpourri is the best. Now before you balk at the idea, let me explain. I am not talking about red and green dyed cedar shavings mixed in with some peach stones and their revolting coordinating synthetic aromas, or some dusty old rose petals that lost their scent some years back. I am talking, naturally, about the good stuff. In my opinion there are only two brands worth buying (Agraria's bitter orange and Santa Maria Novella's blend), but there, of course, will be more; you just have to choose carefully. Don't buy cheap potpourri; buy it from a company that specializes in making scented products, and at the same time you will probably be able to buy a small bottle of "reviver," which you can add as it loses its smell. One of the most depressing things about bowls of potpourri lurking about houses is that they become dusty and neglected. To prevent this from happening, they need to be stirred up quite a bit. I do it as I am passing, whenever I remember, as this brings the fragrance rising back to the surface and once again the potpourri looks as though it is meant to be there rather that just forgotten (it is also really sad when it goes flat).

Potpourri is probably the cheapest way to get a room smelling good. It is like slow-releasing vitamins and it lasts for ages, unlike the candles that usually last about nine hours and cost about the same. Know when to chuck

Know when to chuck out your potpourri; if you don't have a bottle of the revitalizing fluid, there will come a moment when, despite endless churning up, you have had the best of it.

out your potpourri; if you don't have a bottle of the revitalizing fluid, there will come a moment when, despite endless churning up, you have had the best of it, so go and get some more rather than letting it hang around. I do also keep some by the sofa in my sitting room—every now and then it will let out a blast of deliciousness.

Basically anything that is just going to continue to smell good is what you need in your hall, and any heavily scented flowers are a good living alternative to dried potpourri. Tuberoses smell divine and are ideal for the hall, but they are not recommended for bedrooms. Plants are very healthy to have around the home because they take in

the carbon dioxide in the air, but tuberoses do the opposite and so are not good to have in the room in which you sleep. Other scents that would be lovely are freesias (you need lots of them as they look a bit weedy otherwise), hyacinths, lilies and jasmine—jasmine will grow and grow if you look after it properly. I went somewhere the other day where they had two enormous jasmine plants in the drawing room and you could smell them from the moment you walked into the house. Jasmine has the most sophisticated scent, it is not too sweet or even too floral and it takes on the overall smell of the house, which feels reassuringly old-fashioned and sophisticated.

Everything in your bedroom and bathroom should be clean and fresh, so what better things to have than candles and linen spray and something delicious in the bath?

Burning essences and essential oils

The alternative to candles and potpourri is burning essence and essential oils. The burners can be a bit of a nightmare, though, as I have yet to find one that isn't hideously ugly, and I find all that business with the nightlight candle and the bowl of water is just too much like a bit of an effort, if not touching on the side of being New Age and spiritual. They smell fabulous, though, and I should get it together and stop being so disorganized and lazy. For me, the essences work just as well when put on a ring on a light bulb. This is clean and efficient and does not require any freaking out while you are sitting in a restaurant wondering if you left the candle lit. At the moment I am trying to find a sign writer who will come and write on the back of my front door "Candles, keys, lipstick" so I can be reminded every time I leave the house of the important things that I shouldn't forget.

These smells can be very strong and you only ever really smell them when you leave the room and come back in. I have fallen into the trap of putting a few drops onto a bulb, not smelling anything and so putting on some more and then friends arriving and nearly passing out. Essential oils are also excellent in the bath, so are a fabulous little economy—check the bottle because sometimes they are not suitable for the skin. I wouldn't do this with burning essences, but the essential oils are fine once they are mixed with water and they make the bathroom smell fantastic.

Finding the right scent for the right room

There are different scents that are good for different areas of the house, and while most are good everywhere, your mood reflects the smell of a room and vice versa. Just as distinctive smells remind you of places and times in your life, they do in your home too. For example, in your bedroom you will probably want something that is gentle and calming, like a citrus or florals and lavender.

Everything in your bedroom and bathroom should be clean and fresh, so what better things to have than candles and linen spray and something delicious in the bath? Jo Malone, England's premiere perfumer, has always recommended fragrance layering and, of all the rooms in the house, the bathroom is the one to do it in. Candles in themselves are relaxing; in fact, the very act of lighting one sets a tone of calmness and they cast such a gentle light that all this combined with their scent is a very good thing.

What is better than to come home after an awful day and head straight for the sanctuary of your bedroom, light a delicious candle, run a bath filled with yummy oils and then spend an evening getting deeply involved with cuticle creams, ten-minute masks, thick body scrubs and all the rest, followed by some time in a hotel-style fluffy white robe and then getting into a crisply made bed for a film? Or an evening with a good book, or just lying there comatose with hot compresses on your face?

These are perfect little treats, and while I am aware it is only possible to have a completely selfish evening if you are single and don't have a bunch of children to give dinner to, there must be time once they are in bed to indulge yourself, and if you have a husband, he can make the hot compresses for you. Or if that is too much like pushing your luck, he could join in the whole thing. In fact, if you have got a house full of children, or even a house full of the noise of just one baby, this is the time to do all of these things. You must keep time for yourself or you are going to go out of your mind and be no good to anyone.

ME, ME, ME, ME AND HOW TO SPOIL ONESELF

Lavender in a baby's room is lovely. My friend Lucy lights lots of candles in her son's bedroom before she puts him to bed; one is scented and the others are just nightlights. His room is the calmest place in the house and I am sure that it is why he is so good at going to sleep. But listen, I am not an authority on childcare and please don't hold me to it, it's just a suggestion.

A short word on joss sticks. I don't really like them, but, as with many things, there are certainly two categories, the good and the nasty. Fragrance is not really worth economizing on. It is very studenty and a bit "trying to hide the smell of pot" to have that very smoky smell of cheap joss sticks. I find it tickles the inside of my nostrils and it is definitely an irritant, masking other smells. Having said that, joss sticks have progressed somewhat—for starters they are now called things like essence or burning sticks. They come with little dishes and you can get delicious aromas. The only tip that I can really give is that if they are very long, you may need to put them out after a while as they can be really quite potent. I would also keep them for the winter or certainly only for the nighttime in the summer—their smokiness makes them quite heavy for the summer months.

What scent where

According to Jo Malone, fragrance is really no different than color and should be viewed, like color, as a decorating tool and a room is simply incomplete without a good smell. However, just as color is quite terrifying to a lot of people when faced with a blank room, so I imagine is mixing fragrances. As an easy guide Jo suggests that the spices, like orange, cinnamon and sandalwood, are good for libraries, men's dressing rooms and sumptuous drawing

FRAGRANCE IS REALLY NO DIFFERENT THAN COLOR AND SHOULD BE VIEWED, LIKE COLOR, AS A DECORATING TOOL.

rooms. They are the crimsons, ochres and chocolate browns of fragrance; the deep velvets and paisleys. They are also the smells of Christmas and stormy weather; when there is a gale beating against your window, these are the fragrances that you want to have around you, they are just so cozy and warm. If menthol is ice, these are fire.

You could even consider bringing these colors into the room with the scent. It does not mean that if you have a dark red room these are the smells to use; the room may be whitewashed but the atmosphere that you want to create is a warm one, that reflects these colors. As a child, our house always smelled of bitter orange during the winter; the most delicious blend of cinnamon, orange, roses and other good things. I have to confess that cinnamon is a tricky scent for me as it can go the way of peach in that it conjures up tacky tartan decorations and cheap mulled wine mixes. Fake sweet cinnamon is revolting; make sure it is more bitter than sweet or it can get awfully sickly.

Lighter rooms, like chintz-filled drawing rooms or just paler palettes, are more suited to florals like geranium, hyacinth, orange blossom and roses. For bedrooms, choose something along the lines of lily of the valley, lime blossom or even a little violet. But be careful of violet as it can get very old-ladyish, which is not an atmosphere that one wants to promote in the bedroom. It is a delicious smell, but use it sparingly.

Again, there are winter and summer florals. So for a cold winter night you may want to burn a tuberose candle in your bedroom or jasmine; these are much heavier smells that will envelop you. Tuberose fills a room very quickly and can be mixed with a citrus smell such as grapefruit to lift it. Burn a couple of scented candles at the same time to create your own heady mix. Just experiment and if it smells dreadful, open a window and start again. All I suggest is that you do it with confidence. Taste is such a precarious thing—there are no rules. All you need is to be sure of what you like. One of Jo Malone's most delicious blends is amber and lavender, which I was amazed by when I first discovered it. First of all, by the idea of amber smelling of anything and secondly it being combined with something like lavender is quite delicious. I used to wear the body cream as a foundation to gardenia scent. Strike out and have a go.

FAT SATURDAYS

I defy anyone to say she has not had one of these. Even the skinniest of girls complain of bloated stomachs, usually a little wheat intolerance, or even those dreadfully depressing swollen ankles, which really send your legs off kilter. But beyond just feeling fat, they are also low-on-morale days when the world is doing you wrong. These are not the days to go off and try to find the perfect pair of jeans. Avoid all clothes shops with bad lighting in the changing rooms where you are going to be faced with your naked body in your Bridget Jones knickers being down lit, which so beautifully enhances every lump and shadow of cellulite that you didn't realize you had.

Head for beauty instead. Go to any department store and set about spoiling yourself with some new bath oils, scrubs, nail polish (toenails never suffer the same fate as your hips and they rarely get bitten). The joy of not hav-

GO TO ANY DEPARTMENT STORE AND SET ABOUT SPOILING YOURSELF WITH SOME NEW BATH OILS, SCRUBS, NAIL POLISH.

ing to take off your clothes and knowing that when you get home your bathroom is going be almost entirely redecorated with products is almost too much to bear. I know this sounds rather expensive and that Fat Saturdays usually come when your checking account is looking positively anorexic, but you can compromise. If this is the case, just spend a small amount of cash. Come home and sit on your bathroom floor and clean around all the tops of the bottles of lotions that have become clogged up and dusty; chuck out every horrible sample that you have got free with a purchase and never used; wash away all the spilled powder that is all over the makeup, and replace the junk with the new purchases.

I may be insane but I love my bathroom and it is such an easy place to be at the end of a Fat Saturday. Even though it is the smallest room in my flat, I can spend hours fiddling in there. You can get a sparkle up in there more easily than in any other room, because there is no upholstery and it really suits being barefoot, which suits me. For morale this has got to be a good room. Get it smelling delicious and get some order in there. By the time you have finished and all your bottles are standing immaculately on gleaming glass, you will be feeling better. Because it is a pretty mindless task it enables you to think calmly, and as it is completed you will have a sense of order in a room, which will give you a clearer head. You will probably not have thought about eating much either, which helps for a slimmer Monday.

Look to your home

Lightweight bank accounts are great inspirations for the Fat Saturday and while I would like to try to encourage you to find some cash somewhere to spoil yourself with, sometimes it is just not possible. When those irritating people say, "Oh come on, it's only sixty quid, you always have sixty quid in your bank," I find myself murmuring something pathetically. Instead of feeling like a loser, I just feel a bit teenage. So when there really isn't a penny, turn inward on the home.

Clean out the cupboards, but be sure not to be too dramatic (I have found myself with nothing much to spend and nothing to wear). Instead, rearranging what you do have is good for morale. Get the sweaters color coded, and if there seems to be a dearth of clothes in your cupboard, put the sweaters on hangers—they will look delightful and make you feel like you have masses to wear. Organize all the skirts together and all the trousers; start making it efficient. Polish your shoes and get the ones that need repair-

> Attack the chores that you have been putting off and which keep staring at you from the corner of the room. Face them head-on and you will feel absolutely marvelous by the end of the day.

ing out from the black hole at the back and down to the shoe repair. Chuck out the piles of paper and things you have not been quite sure what to do with for three years. If you have not done anything with them yet, you don't need to. Suddenly an area of immaculately clean carpet will appear, sadly ready for the incoming junk, but try and keep it at bay for a while.

Change your bed, too, even if you had clean sheets the day before; at times like these it is a frivolity you can afford, and it will be the perfect preparation for a good evening in with a movie or a book. Taking to your bed at the end of all this is very good for you—after all, feeling miserable is tantamount to being ill. But you need to feel like you deserve it, so try not to get into an unmade bed—v. depressing—or, indeed, into bed at all while the rest of your room looks like downtown Kabul (chaos is no good for morale). Attack the chores that you have been putting off and which keep staring at you from the corner of the room. Face them head-on and you will feel asolutely marvelous by the end of the day.

The fridge

Food is not really my thing. Well, cooking isn't really my thing actually. I have to consult with Rowan every time I need to know anything. When we lived together, he cooked everything and I despaired at the quantity of flat-leaf parsley there was all over the kitchen floor. He regards good food as the ultimate treat and takes huge pleasure in preparing it for himself. Amazingly he is as thin as a rake, which unfairly I am not. He does do crazy things like go off and buy a rabbit, a partridge and something else with far too much fur on it and will make himself some Babette-style feast with it all, which frankly is too scary for me. But what is a brilliant idea from his larder of little luxuries is the emergency dinner when you need some help in the stressed-out department.

One of the particularly good staples to have in the fridge for a rainy day is some good chicken stock, as this will allow you to make a delicious risotto that, provided you are prepared to stir for ten minutes without stopping, will always be delicious. Then there is the jar of confit or pâté, which lasts for ages and takes no amount of effort to get onto a piece of toast. Rowan recommends always keeping a small pot of delicious pâté in the cupboard for those gloomy evenings when you really can't be bothered to cook. Caviar is obviously good for a little morale boost and tastes best when eaten with the least amount of special occasion possible. This is more spoiling than attacking the chores, don't you think?

While the caviar option sounds ridiculous and only for the Imeldas of this world, think again. Without wishing to sound like one of the aforementioned insensitive sorts who don't understand anorexic checking account syndrome, $50 when you are in the doldrums is a good amount to spend on something deeply extravagant. You don't need to be a great chef; just replace the baked beans on the top of your baked potato with some crème fraîche and a small pot of caviar and you will instantly feel better. Eating caviar alone is the best time to get stuck in. You don't have to offer it to anyone else and you are more likely to be able to afford to eat as much as you want.

My idea of a treat is always chocolate or sweets, especially rose and violet creams. I have a sweet tooth like a small child and nothing gives me more pleasure than finding half a bar of chocolate in the cupboard. In fact, at the low points in my life I have retreated to Charbonnel & Walker for half a pound of rose and violet creams.

The last time I did this (I am glad to say it was a long time ago), the boy that had inspired the morale boosting trip to Bond Street invaded my chocolates and movie–style evening quite unannounced, asked if there was any chocolate in the house, polished off the box and then said, "Haven't you got any proper chocolate like a Twix or something?" Uuuuuuuuuuuuuuuurrgh. Men really don't understand chocolate like girls do.

I am certainly of the school that cannot resist an entire box and I long to be someone who can eat sweets and chocolates one at a time and make them last. Lucy (my friend who shares my taste in sweets almost exactly) has had a jar of Gummi Bears in her cupboard for about two years, can still eat snowballs, which sadly I have overeaten and cannot look at any longer, and is really easy to excite over a packet of sour strawberry laces. All reasons enough for her to be a very high-ranking friend. In fact, it is Lucy who started the chocolate treats. She keeps a box of Charbonnel & Walker rose and violets conveniently positioned above her baby's diaper changing table so that when she is faced with a really explosive diaper she just pops one of these scented delights on her tongue to take away some of the pain. I daresay she must rather look forward to these moments as I was surprised to see a child of John's age on such a regular diet of prunes and All Bran!

PHOTOS

The photo pile grows with the inevitability of a Labrador puppy and unless taken in hand from the beginning grows into an out-of-control mess. There is never really the time or the inclination to sit with the scissors and cut and paste for hours into the albums that are lying neglected. So when better to move in on them than when you are short of something to do and need a pick-me-up? Riffling through old holiday snaps and silly pictures of friends is sure to get the old heart beating in time to the rhythm of life again, and if the albums are too much like hard work, plaster the pictures all over the walls. Gather up all the framed photographs from around the house and empty all those photos that you have been looking at for years into the vast collection on the floor. As you go through the pictures, sorting them out for the albums or the walls, you will find excellent replacements. It is always good to see new things around the home and one gets so bored of looking at the same faces all the time. It is really crazy when there are usually loads more kicking around that you never look at. Rotation is as good as redecoration. It is better, in fact, cheaper and quicker.

To sort the photos, if you haven't already, go through them all and write on the back who is in them and where you were together and when. Do not be afraid to throw out any bad ones; I have always felt a bit weird tearing up images of friends but for one's sanity it is a must. Orderly piles will begin to form and from here it will feel altogether less daunting. In fact, at this point you should be feeling quite inspired as you will have looked at quite a few happy and funny memories.

It is easier to start off with putting the pictures you want to have out in the frames. This will get one job done quickly and easily. Never leave the short, sharp tasks until last, for by the end of a long job you won't have the energy, and having completed something quickly and easily, you have that little boost to go on. To get the photograph albums sorted you need to be realistic; like doing the dishes, don't consider doing them all in one fell swoop. Remember: slowly, slowly catchy monkey (this is something my mum always says, and I think this is what she means). You will get a lot more done if you just do them trip by trip and before you know it, you will have done four trips and then seven and then the album will be done and you can move on to the next. This is real celebration time: when those pages are full and you can start to turn them and find more pictures than blank pages. If you really find the big albums hellish to have to tackle, it is much easier to buy the very small ones that take one picture per page. You can have a book a holiday and there is no cutting and arranging that has to be done, which is what takes the time.

Getting the pictures on the walls

This is not everyone's idea of how they want their homes to look, as it can get a bit too teenage, but it can, like everything, be done with a little style. I first did this when I was living in a place that I had not decorated and I couldn't stand the scuffed white walls any longer. I was desperate to make my mark somewhere in the flat. So I covered the hallway, which was tiny, from floor to ceiling with black and white Polaroids and I loved it. I have decorated since then but I will always have them somewhere up on the wall because now people look for themselves all over my kitchen walls. They were just piles of pictures that I had to do something with. The best places to do this are kitchens or bathrooms and the hall, depending on the size. If you have a big hall you are not going to make a big enough impact, but if it is a long narrow hall, you might be able to carry it off. Probably the best way would be to take the wall at the end and plaster it with pictures. The first hall I ever did it in was really like a large vestibule so it was easy. With a larger space, find yourself a patch within it to start on and give yourself room to grow around it.

Before my collection of Polaroids grew large enough to fill a wall, I used to have them stuck in the sides of picture frames. I am extremely fond of this look. It is easy and charming, it doesn't have any of the formality of photograph frames and it has double the love. I am sure you will find these are the pictures of the fun stuff with the people that you really adore hanging out with. Mirrors are especially good for this and I have all the people that I love most stuck around the mirror in my bedroom. They are not always the most beautiful pictures of people either (there is a picture of Rowan that he hates because he doesn't look quite as handsome as he likes to think he is, but it is a look that he has sometimes and it is very endearing). This is a good place for funny old postcards, too; they do well in representing people in the wall of loved ones. This is low commitment, you don't have to go and find a frame and if you get bored of the picture or person in it you can easily put another over the top, which is less easy when they are installed center stage on your grand piano.

Polaroids

Just a quick word on Polaroids, which I love. There are several varieties and all are good. The best thing to have is an old Land camera because you get those fabulously old-fashioned 4½ x 3½-inch prints with a white border. Sadly, mine has now broken and is sitting in the pile of many things to be mended. So I have moved on to more modern apparatus. First up—the Fuji Maxi. I am not sure why it is called maxi when the pictures are positively mini (but perfectly formed). They are best for head shots, as groups of people really get too small and you can hardly make out who is in the picture.

For the mid-range old-style Polaroid, there is the original big square ones that we are most familiar with. I am not crazy about the thick band of white border that goes along the bottom of them, but there is a way around this. Cut along the bottom so you have an even border of white all the way around the photograph, then you can pull it apart up the sides. The back will come away from the front and will now be attached only at the top. Cut a bit of the white tape at the top and then peel it off all the way around and you will be left with a much cooler looking picture. Doing this has never damaged the quality of the photo and it has not deteriorated over time. Having said that, I don't want any angry letters if yours do!

IN THE OFFICE

Even in your office you should work on being surrounded by a good smell. Use something you don't have at home, especially something that you really love, because it will not be long before it reminds you of your working environment whenever you smell it. With good smells you create a positive atmosphere for all those people who are coming into your space. If your office smells good, you will find you are a couple of steps ahead before you have even opened your mouth. Think of the times when you go to another office for a meeting. They are often completely sterile or, worse, really stuffy and hot. Without a scent you have no sense of who you are meeting, they have no personality. Keep your choice light and fresh, a citrus or a

woody scent are both good; you don't want to inspire relaxation in any way.

Other treats in the office are quite obvious, like a
supply of chocolate biscuits. I am also a believer in sometimes picking up a cake for tea for the office; office life can
get so tedious and a break is a really good thing. It also
brings everyone together for a few minutes to chat. I used
to do this once in a while, but you can't do it all the time or
nothing ever gets done and it stops being a treat and starts
becoming a really lazy, fat office. Popsicles in summer are
good too, when everyone is passing out from the heat, and
it encourages good work to a degree. It just makes you feel
so much happier about the work you are doing if there is
an element of care and fun, beyond a health plan and pen-
sion.

The place to be

Beyond treats, though, you should try to make your desk a
good place to be; after all, you do spend the majority of
your time there. Always try to put your stamp where you
can. For example, you will be given a few standard things
in an office, like your pens and pencil cups, but never settle
for standard issue. It is slightly depressing, colored plastic
with ink stains in the bottom along with a couple of old
paper clips left over from the person before. Head to your
nearest stationer and get yourself a Lucite desk set; buy a
bundle of shocking pink pencils and get hold of the pen
that you like. Pens are an expensive thing to invest in because they are just so stealable and you never really hold
on to them unless they are easily identifiable. I always had
these lovely jelly roll pens, which are not terribly serious as
they come in wonderful colors like green, pink, lilac and
silver, all sparkly. Now, this is not black ballpoint, but if

you do your job well, what difference does it make what color you sign your name in, and it certainly doesn't matter how you write your notes. Don't you think that poor old accounts would like to see a bit of iridescent lilac on one of their thousands of invoices for a change?

There are so many things you can get to cheer up your desk, like colored staples and changing the color of your computer screen. This is really actually quite important. How can you possibly look at a gray, black and white screen day in, day out and remain creative? While many people say, "Oooh no, I couldn't read a screen that was a color," it doesn't have to be neon yellow as there are sensible colors that are conducive to concentrating that aren't gray. Green is good, a neutral color that is easy on the eye; navy blue is a lot better than black and so is dark purple. I get a shock now when I see a gray computer screen; it is quite offensive to my eye.

DON'T YOU THINK THAT POOR
OLD ACCOUNTS WOULD LIKE
TO SEE A BIT OF IRIDESCENT
LILAC ON ONE OF THEIR
THOUSANDS OF INVOICES FOR
A CHANGE?

PRESENTS: GIVING AND WRAPPING

PRESENTS: GIVING AND WRAPPING

There are so many occasions that need presents, but the most fun time to give is out of the blue when you fall upon the perfect thing for someone. I find it an absurd idea that I could ever keep something for the six months it is going to take to get to Christmas or a birthday. I am always far too excited to keep it a secret and on the few occasions that I have, it has never paid off. Either I have lost the momentum for the present, the person finds it themselves and buys it (that's the worst) or I have waited so long that I forget about it and give them something else, which is really annoying. When I was fourteen, I found these balloons that had "Happy Birthday Rebecca" on them. It was June and my friend Rebecca's birthday is in December, so I hid them, feeling so pleased with myself. But then I found them in February, kept them and did the same thing the following year. I still have them and Rebecca is about to be thirty; they have probably got latex fatigue by now and won't blow up. So give presents anytime (it's not easy, I know, when they have Happy Birthday all over them, but with other things); it is so great to get a present midyear that it is always worth it.

But remember: giving midyear does not let you off the hook at the official present-giving times. You can find random excuses midyear to give, like when a friend has just got a fabulous new job, when a child has got their exam results, or even when someone you care about is going into a meeting that they have been dreading and it turns out successfully. It is wonderful to be congratulated, but perhaps the best reason to give is just because you saw something great that the person you have in mind would love. The present does not have to be anything dramatic; just remember that giving it is so good for everyone.

So, those are some of the fun times to give. What really stumbles me is Christmas, when there are people to whom you have to give presents who you don't really know terribly well. But even the most difficult to please can be found the right present with a little thought. In fact, it is the difficult people in particular to whom some proper thought should be given. Imagine always getting really dull presents because no one can ever think of what to give you. Everyone loves getting good presents; it is so heart-warming when you realize that someone has thought about your likes and dislikes. Everyone loves to know that they have been thought about and understood. You can offend somebody very easily with a present that you have not thought about or even calculated to upset them.

A present never has to be expensive and throwing money at it does not mean you are going to make the recipient's day. I hate when I am given something that has cost a lot of money where its value means that the person giving it to me did not have to think about it. For example, take all those men whose secretaries buy their wives and their mistresses birthday/anniversary and Christmas presents. Imagine those diamonds and how sad they are, but think of the man who goes and finds you the present that he really wants to give you. The fact that he has deliberated over ideas and chosen something specially for you is just so fabulous. It might have cost only a few dollars but would be so filled with love that it is worth a million. It really is

THE PRESENT DOES NOT HAVE TO BE ANYTHING DRAMATIC; JUST REMEMBER THAT GIVING IT IS SO GOOD FOR EVERYONE.

> It does not necessarily follow that because you don't know much about wine you won't enjoy drinking something delicious.

the thought that counts. That phrase is so overused, and it is often said rather defensively by someone who hasn't given a minute's care or attention to the present they are giving, but it is true—it is the thought that counts.

GIVING WHAT YOU KNOW ABOUT

It is not a ridiculous idea to give wine or spirits to someone who is not necessarily a wine buff. Indeed, if you consider yourself to be something of a sommelier, this is an excellent thing to buy other people; use your expertise in your present giving. I know nothing about wine and fall into a total panic every time I go into a wine shop. I just can't imagine how people know what to do when there are so many varieties from which to choose. I would love to be given some really delicious wine by someone who knew what they were talking about. It does not necessarily follow that because you don't know much about wine you won't enjoy drinking something delicious; wine snobs often think that good wine is wasted on people who are not in the same league of knowledge as themselves and I find it quite irritating. I mean, what chance do we stand without any proper instruction? Share your brilliance.

Presents are easily improved upon with attention to detail. It will make all the difference, for example, if you are going to give a delicious bottle of wine to someone like me who "knows nothing" but would love to, to find a label attached to the bottle (*Alice in Wonderland* style) telling me how long to leave it open for before drinking it, what it should ideally be drunk with and at what temperature. I know this sounds like it would be condescending and awful but it really isn't; it will bring the bottle alive and make the recipient excited about their present because they will know what a treat they have in store for them.

It is true that many men find it very difficult to buy presents. Well, yes, I realize that sounds a bit sexist, and loads of women find it hard too. But I know a lot of men who seem to find it hard to think of presents to give, and especially to girls. But if they went with their knowledge and bought something they knew about, it would be fantastic. Having said that, they should be very careful not to be seen to be giving a present that is more for their own benefit than the lucky recipient's.

By going down the route of what they know about, men are more likely to get that all-important choice right than if they were to walk into a shop and buy something for us to wear. In fact, in those circumstances the odds are stacked very much against them getting it right at all. This does not necessarily apply to all things that men are passionate about—a football-related gift, for example, is not going to get you much more than a very cold shoulder (unless, of course, the woman in your life is equally interested in the subject).

A good illustration of all this is my friend Rowan. Even though I can't cook anything except roast chicken, Rowan (who is a fabulous cook) always gives me cooking things for birthdays and Christmas, as cooking is what he knows about and loves. I really love getting his presents because even though I have to ask him what on earth the thing he is giving me is for, it is lovely to listen to him explain why these particular tongs are the best ones and what they are good for. Subsequently, I have discovered that his presents are always brilliantly useful for my forays into the kitchen.

Making those choices

It is important to remember when buying presents that it is fatal to try to emulate someone else's style. It is a virtually impossible thing to do unless you are very close and understand one another's style intimately or have a common interest, in which case there is nothing better.

The ultimate goal with present giving is to come up with something that is a surprise (not to be confused with shock). I am also always struggling for the look of sheer delight as the paper and ribbon fall to the floor from the present I am giving. I am always quite looking forward to it happening to me, too; that is, getting something that I would never imagine receiving, like a camera when I didn't ask for one, or a knockout pair of shoes. I once was stuck for what to give my mother for her birthday and thought of the present that I would really love to open—a pair of Manolo Blahnik shoes. I knew it would work as a present for her because she would never think of asking for them or buying herself a pair but had always admired them. It would be a surprise and a fabulous luxury. Tell me the name of a girl that does not love to get shoes.

It seems to work that people love getting things they would not think of getting for themselves. My friend Natasha told me this and she is so right. I think of the times when I have been really thrilled with something that I have been given and it is usually something that I would never have thought of buying for myself. It is like getting something great to wear from someone and you suddenly see yourself differently. This is only good when it has come from someone whose style you admire and would love a bit of. It is, of course, a disaster when it comes from someone whose style you don't admire.

This does not apply only to clothes. Natasha is a writer and she loves giving books. Because she is so bright, when you get a book from her it makes you feel really bright too, as she always finds something she thinks you'll enjoy reading. I am sure she flatters people by giving them books so they feel intelligent; at least, I am positive that is what she does with me!

Books are a great flirting tool, the very act of choosing the right book for someone says quite a lot and if flowers say a thousand words (which they don't usually; they say, "Congratulations," "I fancy you," "I'm sorry" or "I'm thinking of you"), think how many a book says. It then tops with "I listened to you" as well (provided you get the right subject). Considering "You never listen" is probably the number one complaint between couples, this really could be quite a good present to give, either from him to her or vice versa.

---

10 good reasons to give

1 For the hell of it
2 Congratulations
3 To cheer up a blue friend
4 To wish them well on a long journey or new life abroad
5 To say that you are sorry
6 To say thank you for almost anything
7 For someone who is sick
8 On moving into a new home
9 Because you saw something that made you think of a friend you haven't seen for ages
10 For their birthday

It is a good idea to keep an open mind about the budget; sometimes you can spend less on something very good and more on something else, so be prepared to move the money around if you need to.

PRESENTS FOR MEN

It is so sad—many men really pull the short straw in the present department, so avoid the desk stuff and the golfing nonsense. And if, for example, you are going to give socks, at least give them in cashmere, which are a total luxury, or give twenty pairs. This strikes me as being a brilliant idea because it means that all the mismatched, wornout socks can be thrown away and with them the boredom of trying to match a pair early in the morning. Instead, the drawer will be filled with new socks that are all matching. Some men have quite strong ideas about whether or not they like long or short socks. There is not much you can do about it if they do, but I hate that moment when a man crosses his legs and you get a view of that hairy gap between his shoes and trousers. It is particularly bad when they are wearing suits. I may sound really prim, but it is in meetings that I find it quite shocking; in fact, that is the only time that it really bothers me.

Very fine cotton socks are super stylish with suits, and if you are ever in Italy go to one of the many sock shops or old-style men's clothing shops that are scattered around. They are so beautiful that it is fun just to see them, as they are a bit like *Are You Being Served?* They are fitted out with all those wonderfully old-fashioned shop fittings, drawer upon drawer of socks and ties in all different colors, weights and sizes with tissue paper in between each one so that when the sales assistant takes them out they all crinkle. Mmmmmmmmmmm. I love specialty shops, and the great thing about this when you do it in Italy is that they are not as nearly as expensive as they would be in Britain and the colors sound so much prettier in Italian.

I have never given any man a tie, ever. They absolutely terrify me. First of all, designer ties are, for the most part, hideous (in fact, the only thing that I think Hermès does badly are their ties), and men should not view their ties as a vehicle to express their wit. Actually, I did give one once but it was a total disaster. It was gray flannel with cream stitching around the edge and I gave it to my friend Nigel who actually handed it back to me as he thought it was too gay, which is probably why I don't really go in for them much. I expect I haven't convinced you that I know what I am talking about in the tie department, but I do think the best ones are very wide. They are quite hard to find and the best places to look are either in the back of your father's cupboard or vintage clothes shops. But it is so much a question of personal style that, ooooooh, I think it is best avoided altogether.

I have started giving the men in my life the old-style toys that I would love to give my godchildren but know that they would hate. Men love toys and I recently found some beautifully made tin cable cars that wind up with a key and move up and down a piece of string. I could have given them to every man I know, all of whom are quite difficult people to buy presents for. Guaranteed successes are Scalextric sets and almost anything that is remote control. I mean, look what men are like with the channel changer: control freaks. The telltale sign for this type of man is when he takes over the building of his children's toys. You know, the type that won't let the children near it until it is finished because they won't do it properly. Another pretty clear indication comes from the father (my friend Garry) who is trying to persuade his wife to get their nine-month-old son a Scalextric set for Christmas. I am glad to say that Jo is collecting one this afternoon for Garry from Joshi (their son).

It is a huge generalization to suggest that all men don't want socks or golf stuff or do all want drills. I have found that men have a pretty good idea about what they want and they seem to fall into all sorts of categories. There are creative and stylish men who know exactly how they want to dress and how they want to have their house looking, so don't even attempt to give them presents for either their wardrobe or the house. Also don't assume that because a friend of yours is gay he wants to dress like a "circus person." This has been a complaint I have had and I feel that I should let it be known on his behalf, as I can imagine that some people see their camp friends as the perfect victims for really grotesque clothes. But then some boys do like to get things to put in their homes because they like good things and don't necessarily have the time to buy them themselves. To ascertain which category the man in question falls into, you just have to have a quick think.

Artistic, stylish or gay (or all three)
This is definitely the most fun man to buy for, but he can equally be one of the hardest, as he does have an opinion. Memberships to museums are really great presents. I have been given a membership to the Tate by my godmother

every year since I was eighteen, and it is fabulous. Such membership lasts a year and brings continuous pleasure to a certain type of person. You can try and go one better than this for the person who is really passionate about art and organize a private view of an exhibition or the reserve collections with the curator. I am not sure that all museums or galleries necessarily do this, but if they don't not do it, it is worth asking. I was once taken to the basement of the Met in New York and shown through the costume department. It was so exciting to see drawers being opened with amazing things inside, from eighteenth-century dresses right up to the present day, and to have them explained to you by an expert is very spoiling. If you just want to give the membership, then attach it to one of those tacky miniature Davids or a Venus de Milo or something.

For another present, there is a day at an old-school barber or spa where the object of your affection can have a close shave and have his nails cut and buffed or have a massage. There are quite a lot of unstylish men who would really benefit from this gift. Be careful, though, for while there are plenty of modern men who would love it, there are also quite a few who would think it was silly or insulting—they would, of course, be the ones who need it most, but presents are about pleasing the receiver, sadly.

Men seem to like getting underwear as much as girls do and the La Perla equivalent seems to be white cotton boxer shorts from Brooks Brothers (according to my very stylish friend Gawain). Choose lightweight for summer and slightly heavier for the chillier months. This is the top stylish underwear for all discerning dressers who insist on understated good quality, but then there are those who are married to their Calvins, so do some research first.

There are creative and stylish men who know exactly how they want to dress and how they want to have their house looking, so don't even attempt to give them presents for either their wardrobe or the house.

The high-testosterone male

Drills seem to come high on their list. They are the male equivalent to a hair dryer; they certainly look the same and, boy, would I love a cordless hair dryer. I have been informed that if anyone is going to take you seriously you want a minimum of 12 volts; anything less than that and you can barely get a brass tack in the wall. You can get drills with flashlights attached for drilling in the dark (e.g., the backs of cupboards; it is not as weird as it sounds). You could also give rallye driving lessons to almost anyone, and the other thing that is really good for all boys of all ages is a day skydiving. This really sorts the men from the boys, or should that be the other way around?

PRESENTS FOR GIRLS

We are really not that complicated. All we want is a surprise in a box with a large ribbon that has taken a certain amount

of care, thought and time. The trap that men fall into when buying girls presents is that they panic and throw money at the problem. They think of all women in the same way, that we all like jewelry, underwear and shoes. Well, we do, but there are other things too. Men cannot get away with that alone, year in and year out. It is, however, always better than a kitchen, which a man once told me he was giving his wife. For me, that would be grounds for divorce and what was it for? I'll tell you what: for her to cook his wretched dinner in—what a nerve. It probably cost $30,000. Just imagine what a fun time he could have had in Cartier, and by December 26 he wouldn't have cared if he ever ate again because she would have shown such delight in his husbandry skills. Furthermore, she would have been the envy of her neighborhood and it would also have been a much more sound investment than all that Formica and chrome. Even better, she rather than he would have owned the present. After all, I imagine the house was in his name. But less ranting—it's time to move on to more practical ideas of what needs to be in that box with the bow around it.

Men take heed

If you are buying for a girlfriend or wife it shouldn't be that hard, but men don't appear to have a clue and, believe me, I have been wrapping men's Christmas presents since I was ten years old. You know what she hates, so that is a start, and you must know what she enjoys doing, and watch out for the things through the year that she admires on other people. I met the most wonderful man the other day who just told me with such sincerity how he delighted in buying his wife presents. She, quite wisely, had armed him with a list of all her measurements almost as soon as they married, from shoes to wrist, and he has the

WE ARE REALLY NOT THAT COMPLICATED. ALL WE WANT IS A SURPRISE IN A BOX WITH A LARGE RIBBON THAT HAS TAKEN A CERTAIN AMOUNT OF CARE, THOUGHT AND TIME.

relevant digits kept safe in his wallet. So every time is a winner. It is terribly disappointing to give a present that does not fit and in England it is such a terribly long time between Christmas and New Year before the shops open again and then it is the sales, which are hellish, and the joy of the gift rather mysteriously loses its magic. Don't take my jewelry, underwear and shoes thing too seriously, they are all truly fantastic things to get, but they must be party-ish. There should be nothing practical or everyday about a present.

The best present I have ever been given is a diamond. I had never imagined that I would ever be given one and had never even really thought that it was something that I particularly wanted. But when I opened the Tiffany box expecting to find a key ring and saw this tiny sparkle, I nearly cried and have worn it ever since. The whole idea of a man in a jewelry shop thinking of you and choosing you a present is just the most divine thing ever. If it ever happens again, I hope I will be as excited the next time as I was then. The reason it worked was because I never in a million years expected it, and that is what you have to do for your wife or girlfriend. She needs to be blown away. On those special occasions when something has happened that warrants a present, spontaneity will give your expensive present that massive extra kick because it wasn't expected. Whoever thought that a wet Wednesday afternoon could be the day that you give someone a golden kick up the arse?

Girls need spoiling as they need always to be reassured that they are at the forefront of a man's mind. Men need to push the boundaries a little each year with what they are giving—it is a dangerous thing to go crazy one year if you know that you will never really be able to match it again. For many women, instead of thinking that they had a bit of a windfall that year, they will think they are clearly less loved the following one. I wonder if that is the bit that confuses men about girls. I know that it is crazy, but in many instances it is true. We are all little girls at heart and long to be revisited by the Christmases of our childhood where we remember what seemed to be a never-ending stream of paper, boxes and surprises.

The best presents really do not have to be expensive. In fact, often when you talk to people, the happiest times they recall are during their poorest. I used to have a boyfriend who didn't have much in the way of cash. He was a brilliant present giver and he gave me one of the best presents that I ever got, the Polaroid Land camera I so lovingly talked about on page 83. He found it in the flea market and being a photographer knew what to look for and that it would work. Similarly, when Natasha was at university, she came home after her boyfriend had taken her to dinner for her birthday and he had had flowers put all over her bedroom lit by candlelight. Her eyes still go a bit misty when she talks about it. Another friend of mine came home once to find her bed had been completely remade in brand-new beautiful sheets and the whole bed had then been tied up with a huge red ribbon (girls really are a sucker for a good bow). Thinking beyond the article is just genius. After all, a pile of linen that you then have to put on the bed is not nearly as fabulous as it being right there in its full glory with the bed covered in rose petals ready to be leaped on. It is the stuff that girls dream of.

Have confidence when you give, and don't underestimate sentiment. If it is genuinely there, you can give anything. I don't know if I am expressing myself properly, but if you go and do something, that means you have had

> The designer gift does not have to be extraordinarily expensive; the smallest of the best is truly romantic.

to think, take time, do some planning and save a bit; for the recipient, it is the best.

The golden rules for giving to the one you love

- First—and generally speaking—girls like anything pretty, all manner of spoiling face creams (watch out for anti-wrinkle, it is a bit of a minefield, unless it is something like Crème de la Mer, in which case you will be heralded for understanding that girls need a pot of something that costs that much for their delicate skin), oils, nail polish, scent. If this is backed up by the fact that you like them wearing it, then you cannot fail. Far too many girls complain that their boyfriends or husbands simply don't notice anything about them, and if you don't, then lie!
- Be careful of scent. This is dodgy ground as it can be a very sexy present and it can just be the worst. If you are going to give scent, you have got to go and choose something totally delicious that reflects the girl you are giving it to. You simply cannot pick it up in an airport while your plane is delayed, unless you are buying her a bottle of the scent she already wears.
- Go for the things that they would never buy for themselves, like beautiful nightgowns. If it is going to make her feel feminine and glorious, then it is good.
- Good music is lovely, too, especially if you have any decent knowledge of it. You will hold a place in the girl's mind—should you want it—every time she plays it. Even if she does not show that much interest in music, everyone needs to have it in their lives and, speaking from experience, if you have a pretty dire collection of CDs, it is usually because you don't know where to begin. This gift has the bonus for a man of being able to buy something that he understands.

- For the all-time mega-surprise, there is the trip. The call at four o'clock saying meet me at the airport, and there you arrive and have your passport and plane ticket put in your hand to be swept away. This is, of course, the most excellent first-wedding-anniversary present. Anything like a trip needs to be given in a very clever way, because you can't possibly manage the box and the bow. A wad of currency in a travel notebook is a pretty good indication that you might be off somewhere. The more foreign the country, the better this is, first because you get more wad for you money and second it still may not be totally obvious where you are going. Scuba diving lessons are extremely romantic and can be given with an Ursula Andress–style bikini. These are major presents and are the once-in-a-lifetime type, so back to solid ground. How about a fireworks display? This was given to a friend of mine by her husband on her birthday. They had dinner at a friend's house and it went off at the end of the garden spelling "Happy Birthday Hunny Bunny." When boys put their minds to it, they can really come up with the goods.

- Girls like toys in the same way that boys do. It just depends on what games they like playing. A bicycle can be fabulous and bring back that childhood rush when you got your first bike under the tree. These sort of large and unwieldy presents MUST be wrapped and you must make sure you are not giving her what *you* want, which is the kiss of death. Cameras, DVDs and MP3s are just as good for girls as they are for boys, and if you are into gadgetry, giving something like this is really fun because you can be as excited about giving it as she will be about receiving it.

- Then, of course, there are the designer labels that girls just dream about getting. Tiffany made a mint with that little blue box. This is proof that the presentation matters so much and sadly it is never something that men are usually terribly good at. The designer gift does not have to be extraordinarily expensive; the smallest of the best is truly romantic. My diamond, for example, is the smallest you can buy at Tiffany, which somehow gives it rather Holly Golightly connotations. I love it more than if it were any bigger, let alone the largest.

- If you have paid any attention to what the girl in your life likes to wear, buying clothes should not be a problem. Think of what you like her wearing, know your own mind before you go in and don't get sidetracked. If you are going to go clothes shopping, then it needs to be for special items like a beautiful party dress or a deliciously spoiling cashmere sweater. If you are nervous, take a sister or best friend for trying things on.

The girls in the office

My friend Glen is really into gift certificates, which is kind of lovely, because he is generous to a fault. I am not talking about something from the Gap; his are for Agent Provocateur, Manolo Blahnik and other luxury things. Although I must say that I am not into gift certificates because they take absolutely no thought or effort whatsoever, what Glen gives is an amazing present in money and spoiling terms. Having said that, presents are not solely about the yield, they are about the thought and care. However, there are moments when the gift certificate thing works; like for the girls in the office. This year, Glen has given them all treatments from a company that comes to your home and does everything from every sort of massage to pedicures, manicures and waxing. I don't imagine that he went for any of the leg waxing, or at least I hope he didn't, but from his point of view it was spectacularly easy. They took his credit card number over the phone and will be sending him the number of gift certificates that he needs, and from the girls' point of view it was fantastically spoiling.

However, if he chooses to do this again I am really hoping that he takes my advice next time. I am not big on slips of paper for presents, so while this may sound spoiled and grabby, I have suggested that the giftt certificate come with a small token gift. It just isn't a present if it is in an envelope. So for the massages, wrap the gift certificate around a bottle of massage oil and give it like that. Or if you want to give a pedicure and manicure, give it with a bottle of the latest nail color from François Nars, easy.

At Christmas, it is a very good thing to give the people who work for you presents—even if you are not their main boss. So if you have an assistant with you at work, it is important to give something. It does not have to be huge, and when I was in the lucky position to have someone looking after me, I did always try to give her something. In fact, the less close you are to the top of the corporate tree, the nicer it is to give, it brings some informality to the office and personal assistants are lifesavers most of the time, or at least mine always were. They had to put up with me screaming around my office looking for something that was usually in my hand. If you have paid any attention to them at all through the year you should have some idea about what they like, after all, you spend more time with them than you do with anyone else. Avoid clothes unless you are very sure; scent is a bit tricky unless you know what they wear, or if they wear something disgusting it might be an idea to splash out on something really good. Even though I am not big on the self-defense presents, they can work for everyone sometimes.

At Christmas, it is a very good thing to give the people who work for you presents— even if you are not their main boss.

Grandmothers

The trouble with grannies is that they are usually down-scaling. They have had more Christmases than anyone else and so have by far the most amount of stuff. But they do need spoiling. My granny was always really difficult to buy for, but then she was quite difficult. She loved candied chestnuts and Shalimar scent, so those were usually my staple presents, although it never felt like she was getting a very good deal. When I was about seven years old, I gave her a copy of my school photo. Unfortunately, I was trying to express some individuality by growing out my bangs, so she handed back the picture telling me that I looked like a boiled egg and that she didn't want it. You've got to admire her honesty, but I remember being completely flabbergasted, not because I was hurt but because I didn't know that you were allowed to do that. I had always been told I had to say thank you very much, even when I hated it.

PRESENTS FOR CHILDREN

Being a godparent is a really fun position to be in. You have a connection with a child whom you love but always hand back. You can therefore have tremendous fun with them because, of course, you do all the things they aren't usually allowed to do, and you can unashamedly buy their affections. Shopping for small godchildren is easy; you simply go to your nearest toy store and buy the toy that comes in the largest box.

Usually anything that makes a lot of noise and has a lot of buttons is pretty successful, though you might want to consider your friendship with the parents. Little girls are different: it seems that as long as it is bubble-gum pink, sparkling and wearable, you are good. That doesn't really change much their whole lives.

My friend Lucy does a brilliant thing for her god-children and I keep meaning to start doing this myself: she gives her godchildren presents on her birthday. It sounds rather odd at first until she explains why, which is that it is quite hard to remember all their birthdays (how many of your godparents ever remembered yours? Hardly any, I bet), so by giving them on *her* birthday, she always remembers and they all get a present somewhere in the middle of the year when they are least expecting it. This giving technique does have an ulterior motive because of course the godchildren remember you, as your present stands out, rather than getting lost among a thousand others at either Christmas or their birthday. Another trick for adoration from your godchildren, or any other children whom you care about, is to always have some lollipops in your pocket. I know that it sounds a bit "child-catchery" (the man with the long scary nose in *Chitty Chitty Bang Bang*), but they absolutely fall at your knees and love you unconditionally until the next time they see you!

Do's and don'ts for children

- Make sure the present comes in a very large box.
- Give anything their parents would never give them.
- Tie sweets and balloons to the top of the presents.
- The wrapped article must look enticing; children do care about how intriguing a parcel looks.
- Make them promise you that they won't send a thank-you letter, and remember to say it in front of their parents or write it on their gift tag.
- Never give anything that you like and think would be wonderful (like old-fashioned toys—they hate them).
- Don't give educational presents.
- Don't start collecting things for them unless they have decided to themselves; it means they know what every present is before they open it.

Christenings

Christenings sort of fill me with dread as far as the presents are concerned. The options are just so dull: when was a single silver teaspoon of any use to anyone? Or one of those pushers (they are those stubby forks with no prongs)? No child has used one of those since the beginning of the last century. It is almost impossible to buy a present for someone that they are truly going to enjoy in eighteen years time, which apart from the spoon and pusher are what a lot of christening presents are expected to do. There are the traditional options—Bibles, crosses, etc.—and then there are the really grand tokens, like shares. I have never really been in that league and they are boring to wrap; to arrive at a celebration with a manila envelope never looks very appealing. So be different; it is especially good to do something a bit mad when you are among slightly richer competition.

Small silver mugs are lovely presents. They are sweet for children to use and are handy in the bathroom in later life for Q-Tips. In fact, they can be used for these almost your entire life. Another idea that I really love is a print of the baby's feet. A friend of mine paints canvases in either pink or blue and then rolls the baby's foot on an ink block and prints it on the canvas. It is a perfect commemorative gift; it is symbolic of one of the child's first steps and the parents love it as those squidgy feet are just so delicious and make a very pleasing graphic on the canvas. A co-godparent of my first godchild gave her a website address and he then bought her a piece of the moon. I am so filled with green-eyed admiration for this man who is one of the genius present givers of our time.

SMALL SILVER MUGS ARE LOVELY PRESENTS. THEY ARE SWEET FOR CHILDREN TO USE AND ARE HANDY IN THE BATHROOM IN LATER LIFE FOR Q-TIPS.

First editions have often been popular gifts, and while I love the idea of giving children lots of good stories which can be read to them before bed, I have never found first editions terribly exciting for children. They can never really enjoy them because they are too precious and by the time they are old enough to handle it, *Alice's Adventures in Wonderland* is probably not what they want to read anyway. But then some of the early classic fairy tales would be lovely to own in later life, and there are plenty of books that could be treasured later.

I would love to give a time capsule that they can open on their twenty-first birthday. The appealing thing about this is that it can be as expensive or cheap as you like. It can include entertaining souvenirs from the year of the child's birth together with some stock certificates for them to cash, which may or may not have made some money. Remember, shares don't have to cost a fortune, since you can spend as much or as little as you want and in twenty-one years quite a lot can happen, even to ten dollars.

10 good christening presents

1 Buy a star.

2 Sponsor a bench in their local park with your god-child's name on it. Now I know that this is tradition-ally something you do for the dead. But, honestly, how useful is a bench once you are gone? I wish so much that someone had done this for me, so that when I was being dragged around the park as a child I would have somewhere to sit down for a mo-ment. How can your parents possibly deny you a quick sit when the bench has been placed there es-pecially for you?

3 Put $100 into a mutual fund that they can't get their hands on until they are twenty-one years old.
4 Plant a tree.
5 Website address.
6 Silver mug with their name on it.
7 Time capsule to be opened on their twenty-first birthday.
8 Picture of their footprints or handprints.
9 Collage of their baby things, like lock of hair, first photograph, picture of their parents and godparents—which will be quite entertaining in twenty years time.
10 For girls, a stone, either semiprecious or precious, that can be set on their twenty-first birthday, when you are richer and they know what they want.

WEDDING PRESENTS

If there's a list, stick to it. So many people don't; they forget that the couple they are buying for have actually gone off and made a list of all the things they really want for their marital home. It is just so easy, they even stick a bit of paper in with the invitation telling you where to go, and for some reason we think that it will be boring for them to receive one of these things. So off we go and buy something hideous that they hate.

Having said that, I never buy from lists. I can't think of a single person whose list I have even gone and looked at; in fact, I have never even seen a wedding list. God, writing this is making me realize there are loads of my friends I haven't even got presents for yet. Never feel bad about being late with presents—ask friends six months into married life what it is they would like now. It seems to be a common theme that what you think you need to equip yourself with for married life and what it turns out that you actually need are quite different, so you can turn your negligence to genius.

It is pretty entertaining to ask friends, recently home from their honeymoon, what their worst presents were (make sure you ask before you give them yours, or you could be in for a shock). They find the worst presents much easier to remember and some of them are very original and funny. The only tragedy is that they are usually really expensive, like the hideous Waterford crystal vase friends of mine were given. So make sure it's not one of yours by avoiding the Welsh carved wooden love spoon, the tartan picnic rug (complete with grass!), thistle paperweights, the three-foot-wide glass bowl engraved with hideous fish and the $4.98 price tag left on the bottom that was a shared present from family members. One bride even received a beauty routine, which I think her husband was more horrified by than she probably was. Likewise, scented candles don't seem to be a very appropriate gift.

This is a good time to band together with some friends so you can increase your spending power and give something really good such as a Ping-Pong table, one of those fantastic espresso machines or any other of those wish-list things that you never really expected to be able to give. The old traditionals like linen and large towels seem to go down on the list as good'uns, but keep them simple. Unless specifically mentioned, leave the crazy patterns and stick to white—there is nothing better. I used to love giving a pair of antique champagne glasses, so that every time the couple had something to celebrate together they had very special glasses with which to do it and they would also commemorate their wedding. If you are not into pooling resources and trying to organize money out of your flaky and disorganized friends, you can do the coffee thing alone. You don't have to have the fancy machine to get a good cup of coffee; an old-style metal espresso pot works perfectly. If you would like to give more than that, you can add the milk frother for cappas and then if you want to go still further, you can give a pair of beautiful breakfast cups (the large ones like the French use).

Of course, all the frivolous kitchen appliances are good—and the more ridiculous, the better. There is the pasta-making machine, the bread maker or some amazingly high-tech Cuisinart. Personally, I would cite those as a half-decent reason for marriage. Home stuff is the best at this time and it would be quite fun to give those mad presents that one associates with one's parents, like the fondue set. After all, weddings are quite kitsch with all those bells and horseshoes.

Try to avoid those motifs and photograph albums with "On Your Wedding Day"–style messages across the front. Although they are quite funny, they are just not the thing. If you are into doing something like that, then fill it with the pictures that you took at the wedding with any others that you managed to get hold of. It takes people years to get their wedding pictures into albums and I bet they rarely see any of the ones their friends took and would probably groan at the thought of having to add them to the pile waiting to be sorted.

Bride's best friend

This honored position does not come along very often, so make the most of it when it does. Can you imagine many things better than your best friend faffing around you with treats the entire time you are getting ready to be married? There are things that are hard to do alone and there are

CAN YOU IMAGINE MANY THINGS BETTER THAN YOUR BEST FRIEND FAFFING AROUND YOU WITH TREATS THE ENTIRE TIME WHILE YOU ARE GETTING READY TO BE MARRIED?

also some things that you don't necessarily want to do with your mother. These areas include choosing beautiful underwear for your honeymoon and talking for hours about the merits of square-cut nails as opposed to rounded and the whole beauty routine.

It is really lovely to put together a present for your friend to take away with her. Aren't honeymoons about being beautiful the entire time? So obviously everything in her toiletries bag should be new. It is a fresh chapter and all needs to be lovely at the beginning of this particular journey. She also needs to feel very special and as there are such few times in life when people do this for you, as the bride's best friend it is an important role to take on. She needs to open her suitcase to find a couple of little surprises wrapped in plenty of tissue paper so it crinkles, and it has got to smell fantastic.

THE FOOD SNOB OR GOOD COOK

Gastronomes sound so funny, they have got to be a good bunch to shop for. Specialty delis are a good hunting ground for this select group. A few pounds of Parmesan is a desirable present; it is pretty stylish and will keep the salad in shaved Parmesan for the rest of the year. It is easy to buy people delicacies that do not end up being terribly expensive. For example, a box of saffron, which is considered a great luxury and highly desirable, is, in reality, a comparatively cheap Christmas present. In fact, food comes under the "cheap luxuries" quite a lot. This is excellent news for anyone going to university for the first time, because as long as they have some Parmesan, good oil and a box of pasta in the cupboard they will have dinner—add some dried chilies to this thoughtful gift and they are set up even better.

IT IS ALWAYS REALLY INTERESTING
TO TALK TO SOMEONE WHO IS
PASSIONATE AND KNOWLEDGEABLE
ABOUT THEIR CHOSEN SUBJECT AND IT
WILL MAKE GIVING YOUR PRESENT MUCH
MORE EXCITING . . .

A tin of pâté de foie gras is a real treat on the day after Christmas in front of the TV. A very good bottle of wine is loved, but you have got to put in some thought, which is the key to its success. It is no good walking in to your local liquor store and picking up any old bottle of wine that is a little more expensive than you would normally go for and think you have done well. Part of the joy is to go to a proper wine merchant and talk to a connoisseur about your selection. He may then advise you to buy a good Cognac or port rather than a bottle of wine. It is always really interesting to talk to someone who is passionate and knowledgeable about their chosen subject and it will make giving your present much more exciting, which is important. It feels rather disappointing to give somebody something that you can't get very worked up about giving.

THE FRIEND OR RELATIVE IN THE HOSPITAL
These are really good presents to give because they can make all the difference to the bedridden. Just think of their situation: they are in a hospital, where the sheets are hard and the whole place stinks. They are away from home and not feeling very chirpy—they need morale boosters. Burn-

ing oil for their light is going to make their surroundings instantly cozier. If they are in a private room, you can take what you like, but if they are in a semiprivate room, you do have to be a little considerate of the other patient. So either make the essence quite subtle or stick to pure lavender. Be aware of their illness, too, because sometimes any smell can make people feel worse. But if your friend or relative is not in that state, then lavender is fabulous as it is a natural sleep enhancer and it is such a fresh smell that it will probably cheer up the rest of the ward as well. Try to avoid cloying scents; they may make patients feel worse.

A baby pillow with a deliciously soft covering is an advance on the miserably hard pillows you get in the hospital. When my friend Isabella had her first child I gave her the two large square pillows from my bed. They are fantastically soft and cozy as they are extremely old and have only about six feathers left in each. It is also really lovely to send an extra pair of pillowcases. The overriding need in the hospital is for pampering—clean and fresh seem to be the things that are most important.

Remember that girls who have just had babies are feeling fat, ugly and in pain. They need luxury. Everyone loves giving baby clothes, so concentrate on the mama by giving an outrageous pair of slippers, some beautiful nail polish, even send in a manicurist, depending on what she feels like. Do not give bath oils and creams; babies hate the smell and if she has had an operation she cannot have scented products in the bath. A Care package of good food always goes down a treat as eating in hospitals is like arriving back at school. Remember that hospitals and even sickrooms at home are frightfully dull. Daytime TV is really not for everyone, so deliver a stack of all the latest magazines, letters with good news and books. Doing

Care packages are really fun to put together and sending presents in the mail feels fantastically old-fashioned, particularly when sending food.

needlepoint is a lovely way to pass the time, if you think they would ever do it. I know it sounds a bit old-ladyish, but I love doing them. Finally, earplugs are good for anyone not in a private room.

THE FRIEND WHO LIVES ABROAD

I have a standard gift for friends who have gone to live abroad and are feeling a little homesick: a box containing a jar of Marmite, a pot of mustard, a box of Tetley's tea bags and some rich tea biscuits, sort of like Queen Mary used to send to the front. I have never really thought about Americans before but I suppose I would put in a jar of Smucker's Goober peanut butter and jelly in a jar, a packet of Twinkies, some Lipton's iced tea mix (lemon flavored, just add water, fresh mint, a lot of lemon juice, fresh orange juice and ice) and French's mustard.

Care packages are really fun to put together and sending presents in the mail feels fantastically old-fashioned, particularly when sending food. It seems to hark back to a time when abroad was really far away and things were harder to get hold of. I am not sure why that is appealing, but it is. I also like the idea of treats being unpacked at the other end. Maybe it is because I was sent away to school, where you miss home and all the things left behind and so you long for a package that will save you from the moussaka with hairs in it that you are going to be having for your tea. For the record, children who are away at school do not want a jar of Marmite, etc. (they should not have left home without that); they require a lot of sweets and chocolates. After I left school I was then sent to Tours in France, which I also hated, and anything that came through the post was completely fabulous. This was followed by a short stint in Paris, also loathed! This is definitely why I have become fanatical about sending people parcels as soon as they leave these shores.

Even if you are excited about being in a new place, it is a lovely thing to receive something from home, particularly if you have been away for a while before you receive it. Parcels that arrive at random mean someone has thought about you and what you might be needing, and everyone loves that when they are far away. Remember that you don't have to stick to food only; books and magazines are good, not to mention anything that was left behind, and a long letter of news and gossip from home. Receiving letters is always wonderful and I love writing them. They need to be very long and packed with who is doing what and general "breaking news"—even when you start writing about people who your friend doesn't know. When people have been away for six months, new people will come into your life and they are good to write about. Your letters become a bit like a soap opera and it means that even though your friend is away, she is not out of the loop—critical.

PRESENTS FROM ABROAD

Abroad is a really good place to find people presents and just to find treats in general. Everything is different from how it is at home, so what better hunting ground. You can go to the most ordinary places in other countries and find excellent bits and pieces to take home. When you are there, you look at souvenirs quite differently. People seem to have stopped bringing home the dolls in national costume; actually, maybe it's time to start that trend again although there aren't many people I can think of who would really appreciate the resurrection of that particular present. Think more of things like a jar of sand from the Caribbean, perfect for cleaning bottles when you get home (see "Domestic Chores," page 246). In France, hardware stores are called *marchands de couleurs* and they are quite exciting shops if you like a combination of specialty shops and a tool for every possible need around the house. My friend Sarita was talking the other night about coming home from her holidays with all sorts of brushes and cleaning products that had very specialized uses. I am not talking about a few cans of Monsieur Moules, but the boxes of Marseilles soap flakes and tins of leather creams that you can't find at home. I don't know why countries abroad have so many more appealing and old-fashioned domestic products than we have at home, but it is a fact of life that they do.

Another valuable tip when you are abroad is to keep an eye open for fabulous packaging, which is often a successful gift just because it is different. When I was in Jamaica once, all of my presents for friends came from the general store. There was a box of oats with the funniest face of a healthy little boy on the front for my friend Cathy, who starts every morning with a bowl of oatmeal. Then there was the Pioneer cocoa powder, which had won the prize for best local product in 1952 and I don't think the can had been redesigned since—and there are all those pepper sauces.

There are, of course, people who love stealing

from hotels. I was marginally shocked the other night when I lifted my knife at a friend's house and found The Grand Hotel stamped on the side of the handle. I asked my neighbor which smart hotel his knife was from; all it had was A1 but it was far too nice to be from a service station. He said that he always took things from hotels. He had even unscrewed a really beautiful old-style steel ashtray from the lift in a hotel in Lebanon (which was quite brave, really, as in that country I think they chop off your hand for stealing). I suppose the combination of steel and lift were just too many indications for him to ignore. He maintained that they made very good and original souvenirs from trips abroad. Please don't take this as a green light; I don't approve of stealing, but I do like the idea of all those cool things—you could always ask to buy them.

TAKING PRESENTS TO DINNER OR HOUSE-WARMING

It is not really very usual to take a present with you to a dinner party, but sometimes it does feel like a good thing to do. It never needs to be anything terribly dramatic; it should really be just a token and because of that it can be a fun thing to buy and give. For example, if you are going to someone's house for the first time or they have just moved into a new place it can sort of double as a house-warming present. There are other times, too, when it is a good idea, like going to your boyfriend/girlfriend's parents' for the first time. It does not have to be done in an oily fashion. In fact, as long as it is just a token and not too over-the-top, it is perfect. In that situation it is also good to do something slightly original; actually, in every situation originality is a good idea. So instead of taking the standard box of brown-nosing chocolates, make them a little different; perhaps

PRESENTS: GIVING AND WRAPPING

take a bar of flavored chocolate (Rococo, my favorite chocolate shop in London, makes black pepper chocolate and Earl Grey chocolate, which even if she is a complete harridan she is going to be intrigued by), and you might win her over for at least as long as it takes to eat it. There is a Jewish tradition at Rosh Hashanah (Jewish New Year) of dipping a piece of apple in honey in the hope of a sweet year. So it is quite common to take delicious pots of honey to people's houses at this time. Although I am not Jewish, it is a tradition that really appeals to me for its charming and generous symbolism, so I have adopted it, year round. Everyone loves honey and you can get such tasty varieties.

If you are taking something delicious to nibble on before dinner, you do have to think quite carefully about the people you are dining with as there are some people who would be rather offended by such an offering, while there are others, like me, who would love it. This is quite a subtle form of self-care. How often has your heart sunk when you have arrived somewhere (starving) and spotted a raw chicken sitting on the kitchen counter? I always forget to buy things for before dinner; I just find "eats" a bit much to have to think about at the end of the day when I am struggling to remember who is actually coming to dinner and if any of them are going to like each other. Well, it's not quite that bad, but I do quite often forget.

Dinner with the wine buffs

I have sometimes found myself in a situation where I am going to dinner with friends who love wine and as a result always know what they want to serve. While this is lovely when I'm there, it always makes me nervous about taking wine. It seems awful to arrive empty-handed and it is a poor excuse to say they know more about wine than I do,

IT IS NOT REALLY VERY USUAL TO TAKE A PRESENT WITH YOU TO A DINNER PARTY, BUT SOMETIMES IT DOES FEEL LIKE A GOOD THING TO DO.

It is good
to take
something
delicious to
have with
coffee,
because then
it is little and
easy and you
aren't
interfering
with dinner.

so I figure that I should think about taking something else. The trouble with this particular couple is that Lucy is one of my best friends and is even more style-obsessed than I am! So I can't dazzle her with a bar of Rococo chocolate, because she is probably the person who told me about it, but it does also make her a really fun person to go and find something for as she will get as excited as I do about a jar of jam that has a really beautiful label.

It is good to take something delicious to have with coffee, because then it is little and easy and you aren't interfering with dinner. This is also the only time that presents should not be wrapped, although presented well, you know, like encased in a little bit of tissue or popped into a cellophane bag or something similar.

FLOWERS

Try to avoid flowers that are not absolutely ready to go into a vase. The boredom of being handed a bunch of flowers that need cutting down and arranging at the moment when you are trying to make sure your guests have a drink, are happy and might get some dinner within the hour is huge. Very often flower stands will have little posies of seasonal flowers like lily of the valley or violets and those are a delight to receive and lovely to give. Actually, it really depends on the flowers. On my birthday a friend of mine, Becca, brought me a bunch of sweet peas picked from her garden. They were one of the loveliest presents I got; garden flowers are a particular treat because they cannot be bought.

Even if you buy "garden roses," at vast expense, they still don't ever come all cut at uneven lengths wrapped in a kitchen towel. My friend Stefan once brought me tulips on Valentine's Day when I was having a party with a friend. My heart sank slightly as I was handed them—the room was packed to bursting point with people jostling drinks and cigarettes, and the thought of getting into the kitchen and finding a vase seemed like a joke. However, somebody did pass me something to put them in and I literally dumped them in this vase of water without even untying the rubber bands. They looked so great, they lasted for a week after the party, long after all the mess and horror had been swept away, and I really loved them and felt so awful for my moment of doubt. As a result, I have decided that tulips are good from the low-maintenance point of view because they have such a fabulously haphazard nature. They rather prefer being left without too much arranging.

You can avoid the having-to-arrange-on-the-spot problem altogether by sending your hostess flowers after the event. Do pay attention to what you are sending and if you have time, go and choose them yourself. This is not always practical and should really be saved for times when you have done something awful and need to have more than a card misspelled by the florist attached. Request no foliage and if you are on a low budget send one sort of flower and less of them rather than a few lovely flowers hidden among a bouquet of junk.

PRESENTS WHEN YOU HAVE BEEN TO STAY WITH FRIENDS

I was once told that it is not "the done thing" to take presents with you when you go to stay with friends, that you must send them afterward. I was quite young at the time and I worried about all of those people who must have thought I didn't know how to behave—for precisely five minutes. I do actually think this is nonsense, and even if it is true I am not sure that there are enough people in the world privy to this ridiculous piece of etiquette information for it to matter. But having said that, there are times when it is so much better to send a present after the event and it is quite fun to do.

The easiest gift to send is a delicious box of chocolates. This requires going down and handpicking (I hate assortments unless I don't really know the person all that well). For Lucy, who I stayed with the other day and for whom it is always extremely fun to get as ridiculous as possible with the wrapping, I went to Rococo and chose all the floral cream chocolates that they have. Lucy and I share a passion for floral creams. I then went and found some dark-chocolate-brown "brown paper" and went home to wrap up the box in the paper and string. I wrote Lucy's name and address in pink and took the box to the post office for as many stamps as I could fit on the outside. Presents in the post are so rare and so exciting. It got the desired effect, I am pleased to say, and if I had arrived at her house and handed them to her it would not have been nearly as luxurious. To start with she would have felt obliged to share them with me, which would not have been very spoiling, and the following week's post would have not had any parcels in it.

I really enjoy doing this the week after the event. But you do have to remember to do it and sometimes it is much easier just to take something with you to avoid this worry. But if you are staying with someone you don't know terribly well, it is very useful to rely on the later delivery because you have some time to work out what might be a good present for them. The only problem I have with this is that I always worry a bit that they might think that I am very rude and the thought hadn't occurred to me to bring them anything.

If you have actually been invited to stay on holiday with friends, the all-time best present you can possibly give them is after the event. Take a stack of pictures while you are there and then commemorate your trip by putting them into an album when you are back home and give it to them. This has all the hallmarks of greatness: you can't buy it, it takes time and it is extremely thoughtful. I have never done it for anyone, but my best friend, Honor, has done it for me and I love it.

WISH LISTS

Every house should have one of these for each person living there. I spiral into a total panic every time someone asks me what I would like for my birthday or Christmas. What on earth do you say? You try to think of the cheapest thing imaginable and then they think that is a boring thing to give. You really want a surprise and do not want to receive the thing that you asked for because then it won't be a surprise. Or you want the person who is asking to guess the thing that you are thinking about and then for it to appear. Of course this is all far too complicated and ends in a row, because you are accused of being difficult.

So, wish lists. The thing about a wish list is that you are not asking anyone for anything; they are for wishes, so you can add absolutely anything you like to it. A Gull Wing Mercedes is perfectly acceptable as is the humblest of nutmeg graters. The joy of a wish list is that you never have to ask for anything ever again; just copy your wish list when anyone asks and give it to them—they will have a broad selection of presents to choose from. It is very healthy to write down actual wishes, too; sometimes they are better in a box!

GIFT WRAPPING

I was once accused of being largely responsible for the global warming crisis, due to the amount of paper that went into the parcel I was giving. But this has not deterred me, particularly because if you give a present that looks wonderful, the opening of it is so much more exciting. Once you have chosen a present for someone, you really want them to derive the maximum amount of pleasure from it. Let's be honest: giving presents is an entirely selfish process. I am often far more excited about the thing I am giving than the poor recipient can ever be—all I really want is to watch them collapse with joy on opening it and, of course, spend at least five minutes telling me how fabulous the wrapping is. Didn't you always decide which presents under the tree you hoped were for you based entirely on what the wrapping looked like (and I am ashamed to admit, the size of the box)?

A brown paper box tied up with string arriving on your doorstep is always exciting, particularly now that letter writing is so underused. Most people only ever receive parking fines and bills in the post, so to get a present is a real treat as well as being fun to send. You can make these boxes look completely irresistible with just the regular brown paper, string and the stamps. Start with driving the lady in the post office crazy by asking her for lots of very small denomination stamps, pack up the box with care so that everything fits in just perfectly and stuff the gaps with bright tissue paper.

Brown paper now comes in colors and there is no need to send your parcel in regular brown, brown paper. I rather like chocolate brown paper, which is extremely smart, especially when wrapped with string, but you have to be careful to write the address in a color that shows up.

There is another trick that I really love. If you use cellophane, you can sprinkle stars between the tissue paper and the cellophane so that when your friend opens the present, stars come tumbling out. I have watched a few horrified hausfraus frown as tiny stars fall into the carpet but, hey, that's quite funny too. Feathers and artificial flowers add a lot of flair to the top of a present. You can use either silk or plastic; it doesn't matter—both will look great. Look out for other small things that can be attached, even lollipops and butterflies on wire. Over-the-top is good, and the more you can fit on the outside of the parcel, the better. Stars on wire make perfect ribbon for the person who cannot tie a decent bow and they look so pretty, like angel barbed wire. Keep a hole puncher handy (you can buy single hole punchers for the professional wrapper) to punch the gift tags and then tie them on with the bow. All

that glitters and sparkles in a present is good; don't get too chic and stylish or it all gets a bit boring: leave that to the jewelers, who do it beautifully.

Ribbons and bows

Layering is very important as it helps to make the unwrapping process last as long as possible. Ribbon is vital, as are the tags. Presents should be ripped open from the center out and only good ribbon should be saved. There is no point in saving paper; it never looks good the second time around and there isn't a war on. Ribbon is recyclable, though, and this is a very good reason always to buy lovely ribbons. It is not very different from buying fabric. I love going to ribbon shops and buying the odd few yards for my ribbon box; they are the adult equivalent to a sweetie shop as everything is so tempting but without the calories. Only use the really good stuff on presents you are giving in your own home because in that way you can retrieve it and pop it back in your box for another day, even if you do need to iron it before the next present.

I recently gave my best friend from school, Reb, her birthday present in a restaurant with one of my best stripy silk wired ribbons around it. A sudden flash of

THE BONUS OF SHOPPING FOR RAG RIBBON IS THAT YOU CAN BUY MANY MORE DIFFERENT COLORS AND VARIETIES THAN YOU CAN USUALLY, AS YOU DON'T NEED MUCH OF EACH.

ghastly wastefulness came over me as I realized that she probably would not be as excited as I was about it and that it was undoubtedly going to end up in the bin when she got home. I was slightly embarrassed by myself, but feel that I have to share this information because it is important to get over such feelings or you will never use your ribbons. Also, as your friend is unwrapping said gift you must never talk about how valuable or wonderful the ribbons are, as it takes the pleasure out of the parcel for the person you are giving it to. I really have to bite my tongue sometimes.

Rag ribbon is one of my favorite ways to economize and be ecologically sound. You know all those little bits of ribbon that you cut off when you have finished tying your bow? Well, they usually go in the bin. One day it suddenly made me rather sad throwing away these beautiful bits of silk and gauze. I started thinking of my great-grandmother, who never threw anything away, ever, and legend has it that one of her desk drawers was labeled "pieces of string too small to do anything with." I am not sure if her pieces were smaller than mine but I wish she were still around. If only she had knotted them all together, they would have made the chicest parcels. So that is what I do with my old bits of ribbon; they all get knotted together and it looks so beautiful. I think that I might start doing this in a more manufactured way.

If you shop for ribbons to tie together in the same way, you have the wonderful opportunity of choosing your colors and you can do this as carefully as you like. For example, if you were feeling patriotic you could wrap a parcel in all different red, white and blue ribbons. The other bonus of shopping for rag ribbon is that you can buy many more different colors and varieties than you can usually, as you don't need much of each.

PRESENTS: GIVING AND WRAPPING

CHILDREN'S WRAPPING

I strongly believe that children should be encouraged to start wrapping presents as early as possible, and if you have children who need occupying during those desperately slow days that are the run up to Christmas, this is quite a good thing to do with them. They can make their own paper by painting those fabulously abstract patterns that they are prone to do, and then they have this way of wrapping with miles and miles of Scotch tape, which is very endearing and impossible to get past while unwrapping.

Pâpier-mâché parcels are something that I am still not sure are more fun to give children or to have them make. I have a feeling that the answer is both, and while there can't be many working adults who would have either the time or the inclination to do this, it is something that is going to have to be left to the children. It is the perfect thing for them to do for one another. They are reminiscent of the Mexican paper donkeys that all the children take in turns to bash with a stick until they break open, spraying them with sweets and party favors.

To make your pâpier-mâché parcel, first blow up a balloon and cover it with layers of pâpier-mâché made by tearing narrow strips of newspaper and gluing with flour-and-water paste. Leave the covered balloon in a warm place to dry and when hard, cut the shell in half, remove the balloon and fill each half of the shell with tiny toys, such as farmyard animals, beaded necklaces, fairy jewelry and obviously the obligatory sweets. Glue the two halves together and cover the join with some more pâpier-mâché to cleverly disguise the seam. Decorate in whatever way you choose.

These wonderful parcels can then double as decorations and they are perfect for Easter because they can be filled so easily with little eggs and those pipe-cleaner chicks. But the thing that I love doing most is having them hang from the curtain rods in front of the windows at breakfast on Christmas Day or from the fireplace near the tree. Breakfast is such a brilliant time for presents as everyone is together in bathrobes, and it is often the only time that you are just family together. Also, sweets at breakfast is the ultimate in treats as you just never imagine that it is a possibility as a child. So what better thing to do for them? They also then have the rest of the day to run off those sugar rushes.

When you are wrapping for children, you have to think back to the days of how stomach-turningly exciting a parcel was. That is why having things on the top of the parcel is much more important for the child than it is for the adult presents. Go for balloons and lollipops, and stick chocolate bugs or cars all over the outside of the parcel. At the till of most toy shops there are inexpensive tiny toys, which can easily be attached to the top of a parcel. I once covered a box with chocolate ladybugs for my god daughter, Jean, inside of which was a pair of ladybug wellies and a ladybug umbrella. The chocolates were a far bigger hit than what was inside.

BREAKFAST IS SUCH A BRILLIANT TIME FOR PRESENTS AS EVERYONE IS TOGETHER IN BATHROBES, AND IT IS OFTEN THE ONLY TIME THAT YOU ARE JUST FAMILY TOGETHER.

10 points about presents

1 They must be given with love and a little excitement.

2 They should be a surprise.

3 They should not hold any strings or incur any costs.

4 They should be entirely frivolous but certainly not useless.

5 Spoiling is good.

6 Exciting is good.

7 A gasp as the box is opened is definitely good.

8 It should be something that they wouldn't buy for themselves.

9 Never give for your own benefit, like a kitchen for the wife, unless you expect to be served with your marching papers.

10 Wrap them up properly.

CONTRACTORS AND STARTING OUT

CONTRACTORS AND STARTING OUT

When I hear friends talking about the problems that they are having with their contractors, my heart sinks. It is always the same problems and they are so easily avoided. The trouble is that you are never prepared for them. We are not taught how to plan a building site or the ways in which contractors work and so the learning process is usually by trial and error. I have done the trial and error route; I don't recommend it, but here is what I have learned.

The thing with contractors is that you cannot leave them to their own devices and expect the job to be finished on time and in the way you expect; you have got to put in the hours of support. There are ways of getting it right and they are fairly straightforward.

Finding a good firm of contractors is quite hard; the best way to get them is by word of mouth. Try to see any previous work if you can, but if they come highly recommended from friends whose standards you trust, this is not always necessary. One of the major bonuses of getting them recommended is that you know who they are and they are less likely to disappear; they also have more at stake if they do a bad job. It is not always advisable to go for the cheapest people around; very often you will find they might quote below anyone else purely to get the job and then the estimate will start creeping up. Of course, the ultimate creep-up in an invoice is when you have to get in new people halfway through a job because the first lot were useless. Generally it is best to go for the middle estimate and the person that you trust and like. Watch out for the foreman driving a Range Rover with a personalized license plate. Everyone has a horror story and just try to make sure that you don't.

You will only get out of your contractors as much as you are prepared to put in. Provide your foreman (head builder) with a detailed specification of works (what you want done) and from that he will be able to give you an accurate estimate of what it is going to cost. At this point it is worth putting in everything you think you would like to do. Then when the estimate arrives and you faint in horror, you can start removing the things you can't afford to have. It is easy to forget that an estimate is a guideline on the cost, so it is important to have a contingency sum for unforeseen structural problems. Hold back about 10 percent of your budget. Hopefully you won't have to use it, but it is quite scary to put down every penny on the estimate; you can get into all sorts of trouble in that way.

TRICKY TIMING

Once you have gone through this with the foreman you must ask him for a schedule of works. Don't push him into working to an unrealistic timetable. Your contractor will give a reasonable amount of time—he is unlikely to want to stay on your job longer than he has to as it is financially beneficial for him to get on to the next job. The trouble often starts when they run over an unattainable deadline and are trying to put men on to your job while they are on an-

YOU WILL ONLY GET OUT OF YOUR CONTRACTORS AS MUCH AS YOU ARE PREPARED TO PUT IN.

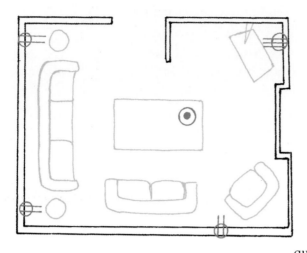

other, so be sure you have got enough time allocated with them, because once that starts happening, your home will never get finished. When you draw up your contract with the contractor you can put in penalty clauses, which means they start to lose money as soon as they run overtime. However, this is quite a hostile way to start a working relationship and it is not watertight, either. As soon as you change your mind on any of the finishes, the contract becomes virtually null and void.

Instead, there are better ways to make sure your contractors are going to finish on time and with everything as you want it. Of course, one of the ways to ensure this is with money. You will be paying in installments and these usually come either in thirds or weekly, depending on your contractor and the arrangements you make with him. To ensure completed work, hold back the last installment plus 5 percent of the total bill until practical completion. Then you can leave 2.5 percent of the entire bill for three months, in case things go wrong after the job has been completed. However, all contractors work differently and you must discuss this before they start so you are both in agreement.

I learned the "cash is king" formula from a small group of crack dealers on Portobello Road in west London, while I was working on a job where the contractors were taking me for a fool, big time. I had actually committed the cardinal sin of bursting into tears on site in front of the foreman and had left to meet Rowan for a morale booster cup of coffee. Rowan was lecturing me about how I should not burst into tears (this was actually making me cry a bit more) in front of someone with whom I am trying to have a professional relationship, particularly where I am supposed to be in charge. I was telling him about how nothing had been done and that my client was refusing to pay the contractors and that this horrible and useless man had shouted at me and asked me when he was getting his money. At that point I became aware there was this guy sitting next to Rowan staring at us. His friend then told him to stop eavesdropping, when he said, "Have you 'eard what's goin' on, she's bin taken for a ride by her builders? Girl—you gotta hold back the money, nobody ever pays us when we don't get done on a job. It's disgusting the way he's treating you." Quite a crowd had gathered and one of them even offered to come round and sort them out. It wasn't until we walked out into the street that Rowan asked me if I had noticed what had been going on inside. I hadn't, so Rowan told me they had all been coming in and out dealing crack. They were so funny and sweet and really cheered me up during quite a low point. The day got better after that and the following week I found a therapist. Avoid the hassle of a nervous breakdown and follow the rules from the beginning, don't let the little things go.

Electrical plans

Among these little things number the wiring. After all, light is pretty important, as is where you put the TV. But despite this sounding like one of the mind-numbingly boring basics, choosing lighting can be exciting if you pay attention to the details. When you first plan a room you must do a furniture layout so you can then do an electrical plan (see

Despite sounding like one of the mind-numbingly boring basics, choosing lighting can be exciting if you pay attention to the details.

page 168). This will mean that you then end up with all your outlets in the right place. You need outlets behind sofas and chairs, you need lots of outlets behind the television, and if you are starting from scratch you can put outlets in the floor in the middle of the room under a chair. Some people always fit their outlets in the floor so they keep the walls clear. In your bedroom, get some outlets and a television socket put in just under the end of your bed, so you can have a television and video there without the horror of trailing wires. Don't put them too far under, though, keep them just under the bed so they are easy to access.

One of the things I always do, and am amazed that more people don't, is put 5-amp outlets wherever I want to put a lamp. This stops you having to grope around in the dark trying to find the switches because they will all turn on at the wall. It is a joy when it works. You can put the lamps on two switches so they don't all turn on at the same time if you don't want.

If you do an electrical plan before anything else, you will be able to have all your wiring behind the walls. I find wires one of the more depressing things to look at and they are a detail that you don't think of until they are pointed out. But once you see surface wiring everywhere and it irritates you, your eye will be drawn to it all the time.

Never leave the outlets to the contractors; they will stick them in the middle of a wall given half a chance. Instead, mark the walls with exactly what you want and where, and put an outlet near the front door so you can get the vacuum out to your car.

People always tell you to put in loads of outlets because they don't cost much and you can never have too many. I am not totally in agreement with this; they actually end up costing quite a lot and they are one of the things that I would recommend not going overboard with as they are really quite ugly. Don't be stingy, though, just be sensible. However, I would recommend the extra telephone line as you never know when you are going to want a computer or fax at home, even if it seems completely unlikely at the moment the electrician is standing in your front room. One of the great joys of life is that you have no idea what is going to happen next, and your life could possibly change so radically that you need a second telephone line.

Layman's plan for working with contractors

1 Make a wish list of all the things you would like to have done and give it to your contractor.

2 Go through his estimate carefully and work out what you can afford to do and what you can't. Don't put every penny of your budget into the estimate; it is bound to increase by the end of the job and that can be as much as 30 percent before anyone even thinks it is outrageous.

3 Agree to the estimate and ask for a schedule of works from your foreman.

4 Draw a floor plan of your space. This can either be done by an architect or on the back of an envelope.

5 Do a furniture plan on the back of the envelope. If it is a big job, the drawing to scale is useful because when you are buying new furniture and stuff you can actually see what fits where with a scale rule.

6 From the furniture plan do an electrical plan, e.g., outlets at either end of the sofa and if you need them put in the floor, and for the television.

7 Mark on the walls where you want all the outlets and switch plates to go.

8 Do a paint schedule, room by room, with the color of

Be straight with your contractors from the beginning; they are professionals and are doing a job.

the paint and whether it is eggshell or flat. It should look like this:

Ceilings: white flat

Cornice: white flat

Walls: screaming pink, eggshell

Woodwork: orange, eggshell

Closets: screaming pink, eggshell

Or whatever your colors are.

9 Check that the paint is the right color when it arrives on site. Once it is on the walls you will have a tough time getting the manufacturer to replace it and pay for someone to put it up.

10 Make sure you never lay your carpets while there are still contractors on site.

GOING STRAIGHT

Be straight with your contractors from the beginning; they are professionals and are doing a job. It is hard when you start out being too friendly and then step back when everything starts to go wrong. To have a good relationship with the contractors it is a good idea to find out all their names, remember them and then use them. Try not to be a nightmare; going to the site every five minutes and interrupting their work classifies as such and don't fuss about mugs and coffee breaks. It is such a cliché.

Organize proper site meetings with the foreman as you would with any other sort of business and go through everything with him then. While you should not change your mind once the job starts, there are going to be things that come up that you will have to discuss and possibly change. If there is something that is bothering you that you would like to change, this is the time to do it and it is always worth discussing. Changes cost money and you really need

CONTRACTORS AND STARTING OUT

to be aware of this. It seems to be the most common shock among people when their invoice arrives and it is 30 percent more than they expected because every time they asked for a wall to be repainted or the cupboards to be changed they didn't think it would cost them. It will and does and it can cost quite a lot because there are domino effects that come with changes. For example, you decide you would like an extra closet built after the others have already been done. A small job it may seem, but it may mean the plumber is going to have to come back to site to move a radiator, the painter is going to have to come back, and certainly the joiner is.

Sites are organized to cost the least amount of money, so the plumber will come in for a day or two and do all the work that he needs to do in one go, the painter will paint everything at one time and the same applies to the electrician. You know how expensive it is for a plumber to come to your house normally, and that is before they have even stepped over the threshold, so the same will apply here.

LISTEN UP

Take advice from your foreman as there are things that he knows about that you should listen to. If he tells you something is not going to work, then it generally isn't. Having said that, there are times when they are lazy and just tell you it's not possible when it is. Question them so you understand fully why you can't do something, but once it is apparent they are talking sense, go with them. I once had some dreadful contractors who were putting picture light plates on the wall. They usually lie flush against the wall and look like light switches without switches, but on this occasion the electrician brought brown plastic boxes that stuck out an inch from the wall and told me that I didn't know what I was talking about. I was nearly in tears again, this time with frustration as I was trying to explain to this thick-headed male chauvinist that I knew exactly what I was talking about. The walls had been beautifully painted and to be told that I had to have these disgusting boxes all over them was just the end.

So I called Dick, my mother's electrician, whom I have known since I was a child. I nearly burst into tears again when he answered, as it was like hearing your mother on the end of the phone when you are somewhere far away and desperately need her to get you out of trouble. He said he knew exactly what I was talking about and would be with me in an hour with the said lights, which he was. For every terrible guy there is a fabulous one. It cost an inordinate amount of money for that hour, but I have to say, I would have paid him anything.

But you want to avoid these sorts of events. This was the perfect example of choosing the wrong contractors. They were supposed to be reasonably cheap, but in the end they were phenomenally expensive and I had agreed to use a firm that I did not know because the architect had worked with them before and he had a very good relationship with them. Every time I tried to go to see the work they had done for some second-rate celebrity (which they never stopped going on about), there was a problem and we couldn't get into the house.

Thinking about it now it was all most odd as the architect had more staff than rooms. One huge learning curve. Handy to have, maybe, but, boy, are they unpleasant while you are on them. The foreman from that job has since gone to live in Barbados, a choice that could not be more suitable. He will really come into his own there with his casual approach to deadlines.

A friend of mine does a really brilliant thing, which is whenever she is working on a project she goes down to site every Friday afternoon with a case of beer and sits and chats to the workmen (don't turn up at the end of the day, as they will all be desperate to leave; if you are going to do this it will have to be on your time, so maybe come in a half hour before the end of day, which is usually about four o'clock). This way she gets to hear about any problems early on because she builds a good relationship with the guys that are working on site, they can talk to her and she can see the progress. It is also so important for people to hear from the person they are working for when things have been done well, and it is just so much better to work for someone whom you know and with whom you have some sort of relationship rather than some bossy cow who flounces around the place sighing about the fact that everyone seems to be on a permanent coffee break.

CONTRACTORS' FAVORITES

- Do not leave anything to your contractor's judgment in the taste department, like where to put the outlets and the light switches. If you do, be prepared to find them in the strangest places. Mark on the wall exactly where you want everything.

- With any changes that you make you must ask them how much it is going to cost and if it is going to add any time to the project. There is nothing they love more than telling you that the reason why the bill has doubled and they are four months late is your own fault.

- If there is anything you have said you will buy, like paint or fittings, you must get them to site on time. There is nothing worse than paying people to sit around waiting for you to get things to them. You must therefore find out on your contractor's schedule of works when he needs things by. Remember that there is very little that does not take six to eight weeks for delivery. Paint takes less, but give yourself a week.

- Do not start choosing paint when the painters are ready to start. You have got to choose carefully what you want and it takes time. It is not really possible for them to paint one room entirely while you flit around choosing the colors for the other rooms. They will want to start on another room while the first coat dries in the first room.

- Remember to ask your contractors if their quote includes paint. If it does it will probably be for the cheapest paint available on the market. If you are planning on using a designer paint it is going to cost you more, so let them know that. They will not be keen because they will probably be making a markup on their paint. They may try to persuade you they can match the color with another brand. If this is the case, be careful: their eye for color is not what they are being employed for.

- This is most important to remember when they start commenting on your choices. I had my confidence knocked by contractors when I first started doing bits of decorating. "Ooow, I wouldn't do that, it's awfully dark." Just don't listen; follow your convictions. Not every room has to be blazing sunshine, and we do live in the age of the electric lightbulb; dark rooms can be wonderful.

- They will have an opinion about eggshell paint, too. They will tell you it is too shiny for the walls. It isn't; it is as shiny as an egg. The truth is they don't like putting it up because it takes longer. The benefit of eggshell is that it will look better for longer, you can clean it and flat paint marks very easily and is absorbent.

- When you get your cans of paint on site, check all of

them. I have had rooms painted in the wrong color and it is hard to get the paint company to pay for someone to repaint the room, even when it is their fault. Mark every can with the room it is for and where it is for (walls, woodwork or ceiling) and then put it in the rooms. Make sure your foreman has a paint schedule stating exactly what color is going where. If you want closet doors to be painted with the walls you must remember to specify this or they will be painted with the woodwork, and this will again cost you money to rectify.

• Whether you are starting from scratch on a whole property or you are just doing one room in your house, it is worth working in the same way with your contracting team. They need the same guidelines from you. Be professional and straightforward from the beginning and you won't run into trouble. Sometimes you can feel embarrassed that you are doing too much with your schedules and drawings of what you want, but don't worry. Your contractor will appreciate it and the most impor-

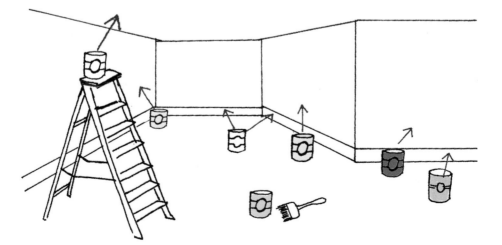

tant thing is that you will end up with what you asked for.

THE GROUND RULES

There are things that you must insist on from the beginning and it is worth going through these ground rules with your foreman before you start.

- First, insist on no smoking on site. This does sound really miserable but it is dangerous and sloppy. So many fires have started from cigarettes falling between floorboards and it is just kind of horrid; it makes the site even dirtier than it is already.
- The workmen should clean up every night before they leave. A good firm of contractors will do this instinctively. My mother taught me this and at first I thought she was just being over the top, which she usually is, but as so often happens she was right. No one can start work every day in a place that looks disgusting. All the tools need to be cleaned and put away every night, all the dust sheets picked up and folded away, all the mugs washed, tea bags in the trash and the entire site vacuumed and ready for work to commence the next morning. Contractors who won't do this will be sloppy and it will be reflected in their work. It is just the same as arriving at your desk first thing in the morning and it looking like chaos; it is really hard to start the day like that. Your builders should have their own vacuum cleaner—don't let them near yours as it will just collapse under the pressure of all the sawdust and old nails.
- And NEVER, EVER lay a carpet until the last contractor has left the site.

11 steps to easier life with your contractors

1 Treat them like professionals.

2 Don't change your mind once you have agreed to something.

3 Set up regular meetings with your foreman and stick to them.

4 Provide your foreman with all the information he needs, when he needs it.

5 State clearly from the beginning anything that you feel strongly about with regard to how the site is run.

6 Trust their judgment.

7 Speak to them as if they are normal people rather than second-class citizens.

8 Morale boosting is good; say when something looks great and show them when you are happy.

9 Don't complain that things have been done wrong until they have been finished, unless they are taking down the wrong wall or something. Instead, wait until your contractor has finished whatever he is doing and then be ruthless.

10 Pay them on time, unless they are doing a bad job. They will always need the money to get the next lot of materials and it is so awful just to hold money back because you can.

11 Never have a fit on site. If there is anything going majorly wrong, work it out privately with your foreman.

Two flower'd-Silk Coats
the same Silk 12 a yard

THE DETAILS

THE DETAILS

If you are completely redoing a place, the architectural details are really important and are worth looking at before you start any renovations. People don't normally want to change these because it just feels like too much of a headache and they envisage huge costs. However, when you are trying to find savings in the horrifying estimate your contractor has handed you, I would always suggest putting the fireplace on hold in favor of the architectural details like the doors, architraves, baseboards and cornices. The thing is, you can easily do the fireplace later, but you cannot easily change the baseboards and cornices. Narrow baseboards are dreadful, as are picture rails (unless you live somewhere like Chatsworth and have huge paintings hanging off them) and small cornices, so watch out for contractors suggesting a nice bit of molding.

It makes me very nervous talking about do's and don'ts. I saw a Milanese apartment in a magazine the other day, which had tiny baseboards with a shadow gap between them and the floor; it looked really beautiful. The moral of all this is that if you are going for high design, you can really do anything that you want.

I very nearly left my flat without cornices as it didn't have them when I moved in and I really had to watch the budget. But my contractor persuaded me to include them and I am so glad he did. I knew the picture rail had to go and I knew that the baseboards had to change, as did the horrible doors covered in beading and the pathetic architraves that had been put in around them. The reasons mine were so awful were that they were not original to the

Victorian building and they were deeply pretentious. There is nothing wrong with not having paneled doors, but there is everything wrong with trying to make them look paneled by stuffing beading all over them. These were the defining details that changed the look of the flat from a moderate place to a really slick one, and I am pleased that I put my money into these areas. You can paint later, you can paint the walls yourself, but first things first and the architectural details are worth changing if they are wrong.

My friend Gawain has just moved into a Victorian house and spent the majority of his budget on taking the 150 years of reapplied paint off the cornicing. It was amazing how thick with paint they were and how fine the detailing was once they had been stripped. It looks like lace now and was really worth all the bother. He then papered the walls with post office brown paper, which cost him virtually nothing. You should be careful of tearing down old cornicing; so many developers have removed it and it is such a shame. Even if you think you want a very modern look in your home and the original details don't work, think twice before removing them. Having said that, you can go to the other extreme, so don't be afraid to take out things that are ugly just because they are old and possibly original to the building. Imagine people in a hundred years time not changing some dodgy do-it-yourself job from the late nineties? Just because it's old doesn't necessarily mean it is good.

DETAILS, DETAILS

It is the details that make all the difference in life. Just as in a person it is the finer things that separates one from another, so the details in a room are what will make it quite special. However, mostly we are brought up to feel these

JUST AS IN A PERSON IT IS THE FINER THINGS THAT SEPARATES ONE FROM ANOTHER, SO THE DETAILS IN A ROOM ARE WHAT WILL MAKE IT QUITE SPECIAL.

are the things that can only be done once the "boring" and more important things have been completed and taken most of one's cash. Leaving the fireplaces and concentrating on the baseboards sounds totally mad but no one will notice there isn't a mantelpiece or working fireplace; they will notice good baseboards and cornices, albeit subconsciously.

Similarly, use a pair of fabulously extravagant glass tiebacks on a pair of unlined linen curtains and they will look infinitely more stylish than those curtains someone spent a fortune on and then couldn't afford the final accessories. Decorating is much like fashion—you can't always have the expensive dress, shoes and bag, but you can often have the clever dress from H&M and the Jimmy Choo shoes. It usually works as well, if not better, and the same applies to a room. It can look terribly tortured if everything is perfect and from the best places. The flea market finds, the tacky wedding present and the splash of a different color are the bits that make a room yours and impossible to copy.

I was once in a beautiful house in the country. It is my friend Matt's parents' house and the place where he grew up. I looked around it to try to work out what it was that made it so perfectly decorated. The first thing I noticed was a funny old lamp with a squiffy lampshade and that was when I learned a huge lesson, which was that it is all those different things that come together to make a look and they take time to create. It is very similar to a good party. It takes a combination of the bright and the beautiful, the fat and the lumpy, and the wits and the intellectuals, to make a really fabulous time, and the same applies in the home.

WORKING OUT YOUR STYLE

Throughout the house there are things you can add and remove all the time and they all carry very different price tags and requirements. Some stand alone and others need to sit well with previous purchases. I bought some turquoise place mats the other day while I was in New York, which was quite a departure for me as last year I hated turquoise and I don't have anything in my house that is that color. All my plates are colors and styles that don't go at all well with these very bright and modern looking frivolities. As a result I haven't actually used them yet and they arrived about six months ago (okay, so it wasn't quite the other day, but it feels like that). But it doesn't matter a jot; I have started looking for things that do go with them and it is so much fun. There is a whole new look to create and it is a bit like reinventing yourself. I can have a whole load of bits that I never thought were my style, and nothing attracts us more than things that are different to the way we see ourselves.

This kind of shopping is also excellent for what I like to call Fat Saturdays (see Fat Saturdays, page 103). You know, those times when your stomach is like a snake's when it has swallowed an ostrich egg. Go off and find great things for the home. Flea markets are a good place to start, for china and glass, pictures, old photography. It takes time, you have to look and look and you will start to find real treasures (see Flea Markets, page 210).

It's all in the mix

Don't be afraid to mix generations and styles. Sometimes it is good to be completely purist, although personally I could never handle it as I would find it far too restricting. It is, in fact, very cool to have good original detailing in a

Decorating is much like fashion—you can't always have the expensive dress, shoes and bag, but you can often have the clever dress from H&M and the Jimmy Choo shoes.

room alongside modern colors and furniture; modern art and antiques have always worked well together. The thing with style is that there are no rules; the whole point of it is not to be doing what the Joneses are. When they tell you the only thing to have on the floor is sisal matting, it is time to rip it out. So whatever you do, do it with confidence, and don't do anything by halves. Don't have skimpy curtains because the material is expensive. Choose much cheaper fabric and use two and a half times the width of the window, or go for it with the really expensive stuff. Never have little scatter cushions on the sofas and chairs; have big soft cushions that you will sink into when you sit down. Whenever possible try always to go for big and luxurious.

If you are nervous of getting it wrong, start off purist and let yourself evolve. There is nothing like stopping when you are in a panic. It happens to me the whole time, usually when I am buying clothes. I have a total confidence crisis and have to go home. Exactly the same thing can happen with rooms.

Having loads of cash to throw at a room does not necessarily mean you are going to get it right either. I have seen so many houses that have got some really beautiful pieces of furniture, like great twentieth-century stuff that I

HAVING LOADS OF CASH TO THROW AT A ROOM DOES NOT NECESSARILY MEAN YOU ARE GOING TO GET IT RIGHT . . .

would give most of my limbs for. But it looks awful because the scale is all wrong or there is too much or too little or not enough of a mix, or it is sitting next to something that doesn't work with it. People can get really anal about furniture and its value; it is no different from the really stylish woman who puts her clothes together well. She is rarely in an entire outfit from the same expensive designer; leave that to the rich woman without a clue. This is another moment to be grateful if you haven't got enough money because you can't possibly fall into this particular trap.

Substance is what a room needs, not clutter or particularly dramatic things. Just make sure that what you do have is comfortable; a badly made sofa will always make a room look awful, like an unmade bed. Funky sofas are going to date very quickly and you will be stuck with whatever fad was going on when you decorated. Choose your upholstery fabric carefully, too. If you have not done anything too dramatic with the sofa covers, you can always change the look of the room really easily with the cushions. I am loath to say don't have patterned sofas, because it can look amazing; it just depends on what you use. However, patterns do have a tendency to go a bit "posh-rental" on you, which is a really bad look.

COLOR

This absolutely terrifies people. Don't let it. I find it easier to choose a color than I do choosing the right white; you can go nuts trying to find the right one. People tend to think that it will be easier to use white, but the trouble is that white can have so many different hues that it becomes confusing. British standard white has a lot of blue in it and so can be cold and then it can be too pink, too gray and too yellow—it is a veritable minefield. Just as you have worked it out, you have to find a coordinate with which to paint the ceiling and the woodwork and you are ready to kill yourself.

If you have any small spaces in your home, fill them with mad colors that you are nervous of committing to in the larger rooms. If you really love a color, it is probably going to look fabulous. Paint the insides of the cupboards something crazy if you want to; it will make you smile even if nobody else ever sees it. Look at choosing good colors for the woodwork, too; so often the window frames and the baseboards get overlooked and are just painted in standard white. But you can do them in colors that look so much cooler and cost exactly the same. These are the details that I really love, the ones where you are just changing the norm, at no extra cost.

Color combinations are also important. For example, I think dark red looks terrible with dead white ceilings and door frames. It is too sharp and kills the warmth of the red, but equally you should be careful of making a feature out of your woodwork. I wouldn't necessarily recommend white walls and red windows. Instead, keep it tonal and you will find that stronger colors can work in these areas. But you must never feel that you have to use strong colors because you feel you have to express yourself and it will make you more interesting or daring. Always do the thing

that works best; it may easily be that a pale color is going to work better than a strong one. Look at each possibility, listen to other peoples' advice, but then ultimately do the thing that you prefer.

Remember that colors tend to come up much darker on the wall, and you won't even really get a sense of this by putting up samples of color before you go ahead. It will darken as it dries but when it is up on four walls, each wall reflects the other, which means the color becomes more intense. The same thing can happen in reverse, too. My friend Cathy wanted to have her kitchen cupboards in the same color that I had painted my bathroom, which is pale sea green. The color came up so much paler on her cupboards that she thought it was the wrong shade, but hers were on one side of a room that had a wall of windows and the rest of the walls were white, so it toned down the color. None of this should put you off. You always get a bit of a surprise when you walk into a room that has just been painted because you are seeing it for the first time and it can be difficult to imagine what it is going to look like beforehand. But stay calm. Just because it doesn't look how you expected doesn't mean you aren't going to love it. And if it is wrong, for goodness sake change it after you have looked at it for a couple of months and realized your error.

For color inspiration, look everywhere; you can even find it in the fishmongers'. The more you look at the colors around you, the easier you will find it to put things together and become quite daring. One of my favorite color combinations is bright green and charcoal gray or chocolate brown, which I have garnered from looking out of the window at trees that are lit by the sun against a stormy sky. The barks are chocolate brown and the stormy

If you really love a color, it is probably going to look fabulous. Paint the insides of the cupboards something crazy if you want to; it will make you smile even if nobody else ever sees it.

sky can sometimes go quite lilac; it is the most beautiful thing to see and very easy to bring into a room. Doing this will get your eye trained very quickly and you will soon learn which colors work well together—and which don't.

LIGHTING

One of the first things that I ever learned about lighting a room was to line the shades in tobacco-colored fabric. Shades lined in white cast a very cold light. People talk so much about not painting a room blue because it is cold. It isn't, but what is cold are the white beacons around the room that are the lampshades. Lampshades can be expensive but they are the thing that will create or destroy an atmosphere.

Having the tobacco lining creates a golden light, which does the most amazing things to your complexion and everyone just looks fabulously good. At night it is very soft and you can see exactly enough of what you need to and none of the bits you don't. I hate being in very harshly lit rooms at night; they should be so much darker in the evening than they are in the daytime. This is especially so when there is a fashion for chiffon, for you do not want to spend the whole evening being backlit.

Some people find that having all their lampshades lined in tobacco does not give them enough light during the day, and if this is the case you could choose something a bit lighter, like champagne. When you are using parchment shades it is impossible to have anything other than white, but try to keep them at least to creamy tones of white. Soft bulbs are another good trick for improving the atmosphere of a room. You can buy peach-tone lightbulbs, which will bring down the light. So if you are not about to change the lampshades, try some of these.

The size of the shades is very important, too, and I am stunned by how many people seem not to notice they have a really beautiful lamp and that they are staring all the time at the fitting, which is so ugly. There are no hard and fast rules about size, and every year I change my mind about what scale I want to have around the place. The easiest are candlestick lamps as you can do absolutely whatever you like with these. Urn-shaped lamps are more difficult because you can very easily either completely drown them or have a shade that looks like a pea on a drum. Don't get in a panic. Remain calm and go with your lamp to a shop that has every size of shade and try them on until you find the shade that sufficiently comes out over the lamp stand. You must make sure it is being fitted properly by the sales assistant. It may be the right size shade but by putting it too low or high over the lamp you will be confused.

Go for color, too. Your lampshades are something that you can really have fun with and they can be changed with the seasons if you want. It is very healthy to keep things moving in a house, particularly between summer and winter.

Halogen

Now a word on halogen lighting: it is to recent years what festoon blinds were to the eighties and sisal matting to the nineties. Property developers seem to think that if they cover the place in low-voltage lighting they can double their money, combined with some hideous hotel-style bathroom and an even more unappealing kitchen. Basically I would recommend avoiding halogen lighting in either your bedroom or your drawing room because it is so harsh. But there are times when it is useful. Bathrooms and kitchens are the perfect places for it, simply because you

LAMPSHADES CAN BE EXPENSIVE BUT THEY ARE THE THING THAT WILL CREATE OR DESTROY AN ATMOSPHERE.

need a lot of light and they are usually quite modern rooms. I have put them in my dining room because I had no available surfaces for lamps, and this is fine because it gives me the light that I need in the daytime and it can be dimmed at night. Halogen lights simply must go on dimmers and make sure your electrician does not leave them buzzing too loudly. Now, according to Dick (the electrician), dimmers buzz and there is not much you can do about it, but you can reduce the buzzing by getting the best quality dimmers or you can go for the extremely expensive option and have an electronic lighting system put through your house.

The other thing with spotlights is that if you don't have enough of them, they cast shadows, which is particularly bad in bathrooms when you are trying to do your makeup. You need side lighting in bathrooms as well or you are going to look very peculiar by the time you leave the house. In kitchens watch out that the cupboard doors don't block their light, which is another irritant that you can discover only on moving in when you can't find anything in the cupboards.

HALLWAYS AND SMALL ROOMS

Any small room should be completely overindulged. Paint it a mad color that you would never dare do anywhere else, light it well and you will turn a non-space into one of your favorites. There is something very *Alice in Wonderland* about moving from a small hall that is covered in crazy wallpaper or a strong color into a large and airy room. Never fall into the trap of thinking that if you paint a small room white it will feel larger; it is a myth. Put a pattern on the wall and your eye will be drawn through it, giving you a greater sense of space, or admit that it is small with the strong color and create a jewel box. This is a good thing to do with small bedrooms: just make them all bed and color.

If you have anything as glamorous as a powder room, or gentlemen's cloakroom as my mother calls it (which always confused me as a child because the only man in our family was my brother and we all used it, including any lady guests that came to the house), cover the walls with pictures and funny letters and poems or news clippings that are of personal interest. It is good for your guests to have something to look at while they are "freshening up."

LIVING ROOMS

The most important thing in your living room is comfort. Never buy a cheap sofa; it is a false economy because sofas are never cheap, really, and if it is uncomfortable, you will always regret it and want to replace it as soon as you can. It is better to have something good, and not upholster it until your funds will allow it or to forgo something else. Make sure your new acquisition is deep enough and filled with a combination of down and feather—about 60 percent feather, 40 percent down. The most luxurious is 100 percent down but you will spend your entire life plumping up the cushions. You need tables beside all the sofas and chairs as it is just such a bore to sit down and have nowhere to put your drink.

There are a few details that are good to have here, like hanging a small picture very low on the wall behind a lamp on a table, which is something I love to do. For little sketches and oils or even small framed photographs it gives the picture perfectly scaled-down surroundings.

When you are working out how you want to lay out your furniture, which can be very difficult given a blank room, bear in mind how people behave in a room.

My mother taught me at a young age never to leave a chair alone, or a shy person will end up sitting there with no one to talk to. Once you look at how the furniture works together in a social environment it will fall into place much more easily. They can look like waiting rooms very quickly, which you really don't want, and this little trick will help you to avoid that. You also have to think about how many people you are going to want in your house at any one time. I have been to plenty of houses where there is just nowhere to sit, which is really miserable. But then I would say that because I am extremely lazy and am not keen on standing for very long.

Now, I am also very enthusiastic on having window shades in my sitting room rather than curtains as curtains are expensive and they cut out the light. Sometimes they are lovely and people like having them, particularly to close out the cold winter nights, and I agree there is something lovely about turning on all the lights in a room and drawing the curtains on a cold evening. But during the day being able to have the most amount of light possible is a joy. Furthermore, shades cost a tenth of the price and are much slicker than all the bulk of curtains.

A neutral palette on the walls is good for your sitting room; introduce color by way of the upholstery and accessories. One of the things that always struck me as a child was that in the summer our houses (we moved a lot, rather than having loads of houses at one time) often felt too wintry because my mother liked strong colors and velvet curtains. Getting the level of sunlight right is a hard thing to overcome because in the winter you don't want your home to look like a beach house, but with a neutral color on the walls you can change the vibe with the seasons. Have dark blinds made for the winter months and

ONCE YOU LOOK AT HOW THE FURNITURE WORKS TOGETHER IN A SOCIAL ENVIRONMENT IT WILL FALL INTO PLACE MUCH MORE EASILY.

then switch them for linen come the spring. Having lighter weight blinds immediately changes the atmosphere because more light is then allowed into the room. Of course, getting the balance right is always tricky because in the summer the strong sunlight then floods the room too much, but by changing back to the winter blinds all the light is blocked out completely. How fickle it is.

If you have upholstered your sofas in dark colors, have an additional set of slipcovers made in heavy white cotton. Now, this is more expensive than the blinds, but there is something spoiling and extravagant about white upholstery that is quite irresistible. Shop around and see if you can get a deal on an extra set when you purchase a sofa, because it is possible for the extra set to cost half as much again.

One of the joys about slipcovers is that they can just go in the machine when they get dirty and the more haphazard and ill-fitting they look, the better. It is unwise to put a slipcover on a chair or sofa that does not have a seat cushion—you need the cushion to hold down the cover. With these two changes you will completely alter the dynamic of the room; suddenly the colors of the cushions and the walls will work entirely differently.

KITCHENS

These are expensive and I always have a bit of a problem spending a lot of money on my kitchen, because while I want it to look good, it is not an area that I am terribly interested in. There are ways around the off-the-shelf kitchen and the place to start is by looking at the work surfaces that are available from the big companies. I always have wood, which is inexpensive and inoffensive, and then I have always, on the recommendation of my contractors, bought ready-made shelving for the cupboards and had doors made and painted a color that I want. This seems to be a pretty good compromise. I hate all those little corner shelves for the spices and stuff but I do like to have some open shelving. In fact, I am a big fan of decorating with accessories and rows of clean glasses and piles of plates and bowls are just so great to look at. This really only works with the stuff you use regularly because if you are not taking them on and off the shelves they are going to get very dusty and even greasy if you cook a lot. I find now that I hardly ever look in the cupboards and that I only use the things that I can see.

The thing that I really hate when I go to other people's kitchens is that sterile, "just arrived out of a box" look. You want your kitchen to have a little more character than that. Buy up old storage jars for your cereal, risotto rice and other dry store bits and pieces. The ones I like the best are the French jars made of dark green glass; you'll find them in flea markets or fancy kitchen shops.

Planning the layout

Be careful when you are working out the layout of your kitchen. Space often dictates (certainly for me it has as my kitchens have always been tiny), but I do realize that for many it is the hub of the home. Whether the room is large or small you must think about how you use the space. Central to this ethos is the position of the dishwasher. Keep it near the sink and if your kitchen is open plan with a carpeted dining room, make sure the dishwasher is nowhere near it. It won't be long before the carpet is covered in stains from missing the machine when stacking your plates at the end of a meal. Come and see mine for details.

You need a lot of space around your sink, too; never put one up against a wall, it will drive you crazy. And if your kitchen is small, don't have a tall fridge or combined fridge-freezer or you will be wasting a lot of counter space. Instead, put them side by side. In Rowan's kitchen, the girl who designed it for him did something really brilliant—he has a freestanding unit (with space at either end of it), which houses his sink and has a slate top and front. From the front you can't see that there is a dishwasher and a cupboard for all Rowan's products because they are at either end, which is such a slick detail. Of course, these niceties are dictated by the sort of space you have to play with, but they are worth bearing in mind when planning.

We live very much in the moment of the open-plan kitchen. In cities this is usually due to the price of space and in the country it is usually because that is where everyone hangs out. You want to be very careful of having it too open plan, though; let's face it, how often do you want to be sitting and looking at the kitchen sink of an evening? Personally, I never, ever do. There are ways you can keep it semi-open, which is what I have done at home because a structural problem meant I couldn't take down as much wall as I originally wanted, but now I am really thrilled that I couldn't. When I am sitting at the dining table I feel like I am in the extended part of the kitchen, but when I am at the other end of the room sitting on a sofa I cannot see the kitchen at all. I would suggest you think about this if you are ever in that fever of pulling down every wall in the place to try and get as much square footage in one room as possible.

BEDROOMS

If you want to, you can change the look of your bedroom every time you change your bed. I really like the idea of having a neutral bedroom and then having a different thing going on my bed whenever I feel like it. In practice I actually have flowers all over my bedroom walls and still keep changing my bed, but not so dramatically. It does not take very long to collect different quilts, sheets and blankets if you keep an eye out for them. I have managed to get quite a lot of hand-me-downs off my mother; anything good I snap up. Even if I don't necessarily like the patterns much, they are always really soft and I have been rewarded for this; suddenly the orange and pink daisies that I thought were pretty awful are perfect for the 1970s Palm Beach look. They are now one of my favorite things.

With old linen you can mix sheets and pillow-cases. If you have not got a big collection of bed linen, start with pillowcases and then sheets, and keep an eye open for interesting quilts that you can add for color and pattern. Old tablecloths are beautiful, although some of them have so much fine embroidery on them that you would never want to use them on a table, so put them over your bed instead. Don't ever have those heavy bedspreads that go over your pillows; they are so heavy and spend their lives on the floor. It is much more inviting to see the pillows on a bed—it just makes you want to jump on it.

The softer, the better

There are many little details that can be added to beds, which make a huge difference to the way they look and the way they feel. I am not sure I am going to be able to swing everyone around to all of my ways of thinking, because sheets and blankets are my favorite thing. Maybe not the world's first choice, but I happen to think that blankets edged in satin are just the best. Finding some satin in the morning on which to stroke your toe is one of life's simple pleasures. And as for pillows—you need lots of them, and I don't mean cushions. You don't want any upholstery fabric anywhere near your bed, maybe on your headboard and valance, but certainly not on top. Everything must be soft so you can totally sink into your bed.

I cannot recommend more highly two large square pillows with two long pillows in front: you have always got to be able to throw yourself (or be thrown) onto your bed without cracking your head on either the wall or your headboard. There is an alternative to this and that is four long pillows, but it is not as satisfactory as you will always have to move one to read and such stuff. Having square pillows allows you to be more adventurous with your linen. Despite my phobia about mismatching sheets, I think it is lovely to have a melange of antique linen and if you have a set of sheets that don't include square pillowcases then you can always use a pair of plain old white ones, which will look glorious.

Now, about the "no cushions," the reason that I am so against them is that they can get dirty and are too hard. Cushion covers do not get washed once a week, unlike sheets, and they spend their time either on the floor or on your pillow, which isn't a very pleasant thought. Think of those weekend supplement pictures of super enlarged carpet mites. But more to the point, upholstery fabric is not soft on your skin, and they are always placed in diamond shapes across the bed in a fabric to match the curtains. Please don't do it, even when your curtain maker tells you there is some fabric left over and she could make some cushions for you. Please, they are right next to the plaited tiebacks on the hate list. Even Kelly Hoppen has realized that too many cushions on a bed is bad for your sex life and she is the *principessa* of stacking cushions on beds.

BATHROOMS

Bathrooms are so often neglected in the decoration of a place, which I suppose is because one can only think that changing it is going to be hideously expensive. If you are buying a property and the bathroom is disgusting, try to budget to change it. It will never be a waste of money as you will increase its value dramatically if you have a great bathroom. But more important, you will actually enjoy having a bath (I just don't feel clean if I come out of a room that has got scuzzy carpet on the floor and a low plastic bath, with bad lighting and not much hot water). This is the cliché by which the rest of the world views Britain's bathrooms and unfortunately it is a little too close to the truth. I was once lectured at dinner by a German about the fact that the English all had terrible showers and this was even though he hadn't been in England for about twenty years. I tried to defend us but without much success. He had a crack at the food and coffee, too—and our battery cows. I tried to explain that we didn't have battery cows, they are chickens, but he wouldn't listen!

I have a very simple formula for bathrooms. It is not rocket science but you would be amazed by how many comments it gets. I have done this twice with my own bathrooms, the first of which was a windowless $3\frac{1}{2}$ by 7 foot box. I don't think you can get a room smaller than that; any smaller and it becomes a closet. It is safe to say that it had no redeeming features, and it was not helped by the hanging lightbulb, the avocado linoleum on the floor

I THINK IT IS LOVELY TO HAVE A MELANGE OF ANTIQUE LINEN AND IF YOU HAVE A SET OF SHEETS THAT DON'T INCLUDE SQUARE PILLOWCASES THEN YOU CAN ALWAYS USE A PAIR OF PLAIN OLD WHITE ONES, WHICH WILL LOOK GLORIOUS.

or the tiny plastic bath. My mother, who like all mothers likes to give a lot of opinions, and especially strives to come up with something that you haven't thought of, suggested we put in a window, but the scaffolding needed was going to cost more than the whole budget for the flat. So that was out. I hit on another plan and by the time I had finished, people were actually commenting on how much they loved my bathroom. So here is the route:

1 Fill it with light, use halogen spots and wall-mounted lights (see Lighting for details, page 190).

2 You will be dictated to a bit by pipes, but if the room is rectangular try to get the bath along the short wall. This will make the space more square.

3 Avoid having the loo right opposite the door. Of all the things to be the first thing you see, the loo is not the one.

4 If the bathroom is really tiny, think about a Victorian footed bath—seeing underneath it will create the illusion of more space.

5 Tile the walls to around shoulder height in white ceramic tiles. Choose whichever shape you prefer. I like the rectangular ones put up like bricks (not beveled).

6 Paint above the tiles in a color that you love. Wallpaper works too.

7 Tile the floor in something different to the walls and try to have something that is not as slippery as glazed ceramic tiles.

8 Put up plenty of shelving near the bath for oils and scrubs.

9 Put up plenty of shelving around the basin for creams and makeup.

10 Put good stuff on the walls. Don't think you should not put your best things in the bathroom; it is, after all, the

. . . THE CUSHIONS ARE NOT SUPPOSED TO PROP YOU UP, THEY ARE SUPPOSED TO DRAW YOU IN AND ENVELOP YOU.

one room where you lie back and stare at the wall, so you might as well have something cool to look at.

THE FUN STUFF

This is the lamps and the lampshades, what sort of door-knobs to have and the ashtrays. Even if you don't smoke, you need them. I often use mine for odd lip glosses or cuticle cream; I mean they just roll around otherwise and you always need that stuff handy. Likewise, old cigarette boxes are great for keeping manicure sets in. Don't you find yourself wanting to do all that stuff while you are watching TV, and so you might as well keep the equipment handy? All these things take a while to collect, so don't panic that your home isn't looking "à point" instantly—it can't possibly.

If you are getting in a twit about what color the sofa cushions should be, forget about them for a while. While such details are important, they have another great quality: they can wait. It doesn't matter if there aren't any cushions on your sofa for six months, but it really does matter when you have rushed out to find something and settled for the best you could find. *Never* do that, you will always regret it, because almost the instant they are on the sofa you will see the thing that you really want. Make sure, too, that the cushions you get are really soft, as there is

nothing worse than leaning back into a sofa and being halted halfway; the cushions are not supposed to prop you up, they are supposed to draw you in and envelop you. Also, when you plump up all the cushions don't put them on the back of the sofa—that look is so weird and slightly "old people's home" in style—and don't sit them in diamonds either. Sorry to be a fascist but those are just the two things that I can't cope with in life. You need to have big, fat, juicy, down cushions in the corners of your sofas and then smaller plump ones in the middle. If you ever find yourself chucking cushions on the floor when you sit on the sofa, you have got the wrong cushions.

Upholstered furniture

When you are choosing the colors and patterns for your sofa and chairs you can be pretty free, especially if you have kept to a fairly neutral palette in the rest of the room. Personally I like using quite dark and strong colors on sofas in my living spaces as they are a brilliant backdrop for sharp colors and they are practical.

Provided your upholstered pieces are in the moveable accessories line rather than built in, theoretically they are always disposable. Naturally, simply knowing this means you will rarely tire of them because they don't carry any commitment problems—sort of like friend versus boyfriend.

Pulling power

Curtains, however, are expensive, which means you feel like you mustn't get it wrong because you are going to have to have them forever. They cost a whole lot of money, take yard upon yard of fabric and keep out most of the light. The temptation then is to go for the simplest option, which is usually the most boring. The answer to all this is that you needn't feel that you have to sink all your money into the curtains if you can't really afford them. Go for window shades instead. I love having shades, especially those made out of my own choice of fabric. You need very little material and they are just so versatile: they can block out the white sky, keep the sun out of your eyes, or just let all the light flood in. Because they move up and down rather than from side to side it is much easier to get what you want out of them.

You can make window shades so they are slightly transparent, which is perfect for a bathroom, say, as you still have the light but not the neighbors. Or use a heavier fabric, which blocks out the light altogether; this is probably the best for a bedroom.

FILL UP YOUR SOFAS WITH BIG, FAT, JUICY, DOWN CUSHIONS IN THE CORNERS AND ADD SMALLER PLUMP ONES IN THE MIDDLE.

Points on details

- They must not be overlooked.

- They need to be both frivolous and practical in equal measure.

- When culling your contractor's estimate, be careful not to pull out all of the details; some can go but others must stay, even if it means losing a couple of the big things.

- They need time. Never expect to move into a new home and have everything just so. It will look forced.

- Some of the accessories you add to your house will be"finds": you won't necessarily know what they are until you stumble across them, and don't try to.

- Be prepared to spend a fortune on some accessories and virtually nothing on others; never do anything in moderation.

- Details in the home are very often simply styling in the way you do things, from the way you serve coffee to the way you make your bed.

- Not all the details in your house need to be glaringly obvious. In fact, very often they aren't and either they remain things that only give you pleasure (very important) or, despite remaining unremarked on by your friends, they will ultimately add enormously to the overall look/atmosphere in your home.

- Don't overdetail as it can become quite overpowering.

- Don't ever do something for the sake of it. You have got to love it.

FLEA MARKETS AND ANTIQUE SHOPS

FLEA MARKETS AND ANTIQUE SHOPS

Marketeering is an essential part of the building of the good home; if you do it regularly, you get your eye in and the more frequently you go, the better prices you get. As you continue to potter around the same markets and junk shops, you will get to know the dealers, which is completely lovely as they are always ready for a gossip and a coffee and you will learn things along the way too.

With everything you buy you will have a memory. I realize this sounds really cheesy and like sentimental claptrap, but it is true. I remember hearing my mum talking to someone about things she had bought. "Oh, do you remember we bought that together fifteen years ago in such and such?" I was always staggered, as I didn't have fifteen years in my own personal history to go back and I secretly longed to be able to start talking about doing things so long ago. But I have started to realize that I can do it now, as there are things that I bought ten years ago, like my gray dessert plates, that I love. I couldn't afford them at the time, but Meredith, whom I worked for and was shopping with (we would often go as part of general office research), bought them for me and I paid her back each week until my debt was clear.

Sometimes with things you can't really afford, it is worth finding a way to pay for them. You will instinctively know if you really want to buy an object or not because usually if you can't afford it you don't think about it again. But every now and then there is something you know that you must have even though you can't really afford it, and you start mentally searching for the money. The few times that I have done this I have managed to find a way and I still have the things and they were all good purchases, most of which have doubled in value. I have an oil painting of some Arum lillies that I bought from a dealer for some vast amount, which I really did not have sitting in my checking account. So I paid for it on the drip (be careful of too many drips; they can turn into a waterfall without too much effort). I still love this painting—a lot—and when I brokered the deal, it can't have been great for the dealers, for they gave me a pound to go and buy a lottery ticket in the hope it might speed up the payment on the picture.

If you buy from specialists, you will learn a lot as you go. Don't make the mistake of thinking that all dealers are trying to rip you off or, worse, don't know what they have got. It is both foolish and rude and they hate it.

CHINA

Buying china in flea markets can lead to a lifetime of collecting the same pattern for a dinner service. There are people who do this and they get very excited when they find a piece and have all their friends and relatives looking out for it. They are the same people who paw over jigsaw puzzles. Personally, I have never had the patience; can you imagine how bored you would be of the pattern by the time you had found enough to have a friend for tea? I mean, you would want to commit hara-kiri with one of the shards should

anyone ever break a piece. It is really not worth the joy that moment brings when you find the sugar bowl during a chance visit to a junk shop in some seaside town.

A mixture of plates can look beautiful on a table, although I would always try to base my collection on a theme or it can get to be too much of a hodgepodge. For example, collect anything with roses or blue and white, but any pattern—you could even do anything with crests on. Single plates sell very cheaply, so this is a good way to start getting together plates for your home. There is nothing wrong with editing as you go, either. You may find that to start with you buy some that are quite third-rate but you need to eat off something, so keep them until they are replaced with the better find. You will have to be patient. I collected coffee cans when I first started buying. I am not sure that I really had the patience for it and my collection is pretty haphazard. The mistake I made was that I was not really strict enough with myself, so there is no fluidity among them. If you want matching sets it is quite easy to find twelve plates, especially of the dessert set variety. One of the first things I bought for my home (which I then didn't have) was the aforementioned set of gray dessert plates.

You must buy well; some junky stuff is good, but in moderation. It is hard to go out in search of things, so look with an open mind and fabulous things will cross your path. It is much harder if you go antiquing with a strict shopping list of what you want to find.

Watch out for . . .

When you are looking at china, look for damage. When I first started shopping I never used to; if I liked it, I bought it. I am not sure there is anything that I wouldn't have bought, but I might have got a better price. Don't worry about staining; once you get home this can be removed with a good soak in a bucket of detergent. Big serving plates are an easy addition if you are keen on the magpie-style dinner service; you will always find these in funny little antique shops and it really does not matter if they don't match the rest of your china.

Worse than cracks in china are any signs of restoration. This is easy to miss unless you know what you are looking for. When broken china is restored, the repaired cracks are painted over with a matte white finish to hide them. Unless you love the item and are prepared to use it only for display purposes, you should not buy it. You can't wash it as eventually the glue will dissolve and you will be left with a broken plate.

KITCHENWARE

Kitchenware has been extremely popular for years. I used to know an American dealer who would come to England and just buy dozens of breadboards and bread bins. It was staggering to see and she would return to the States and sell them almost as soon as she arrived home. I have never been very turned on by spending fortunes on cooking gear;

I mean there are just so many other things that I would rather be spending money on. In fact, my kitchen is entirely equipped by my granny, who sadly died just before I moved into my first flat. All her saucepans, wooden spoons, cocottes, etc., are with me, together with her very early Moulinex coffee grinder, which I love. This was all fabulous until I found out that aluminium saucepans have been linked with Alzheimer's disease.

There are good things to be found that aren't quite as bad for your health, like any of the enamel stuff (just make sure that it isn't chipped; I think that might be poisonous, too), and kitchen bowls; they are just so much more beautiful when they are old, not to mention cheaper. When it comes to kitchenware being cheaper, for me this is really attractive. Kitchens can get that "just married" look, you know, the slightly smug "we got *everything* on our wedding list, even the lemon zester." I honestly find it quite unappealing, though I used to love going into kitchen shops with my mother and would always be persuading her to buy things exactly like that lemon zester, which promises to revolutionize your life. But now, slotting into a stereotype with the right sort of olive oil and the must-have saltcellar with a wooden tray really turns me off, so the flea market is a good place—they don't do wedding lists either! Listen, don't take me at my word. These wretched social stereotypes do panic me a bit, and if you get everything in the market, like all those tins that say sugar and flour and currants in French, you just fall into another little box.

Dishcloths are beautiful and can be found unused. I am not sure why there is so much old linen that never got unpacked. Perhaps it has something to do with people's trousseaux; maybe they never got married and had drawers full of all this stuff that never saw the light of day. Some of them make very stylish napkins for kitchen dinners or even TV suppers, and because they are so much larger than a napkin they really cover you up.

There is a small tip about dishcloths that is very useful: buy them in only one color—white or beige, for example—which means they can always go in the washing machine at the same time, in a hot wash with bleach if necessary. I have a tartan dishcloth that is the black sheep of the dishcloths as it is always waiting to go in the wash but there are always more whites that it can't go in with, so it is a real burden around the kitchen.

GLASS

Glass is a joy to buy at markets; I have found real treasures. I started by collecting amethyst glass for my mother at a market in west London. You will find things that you cannot buy any longer. The Victorians, in particular, had a glass for everything: cordial glasses, rummers, glasses for syllabubs and jellies, heavy-based shot glasses for slamming on the table. They all sound so delicious and can be used for so many things. Be careful of ending up with too many single glasses, though. Unless you have a lot of bedrooms (they can always be put beside beds), they are kind of useless in bulk, so be controlled. Look out for mini-highballs (they are like Moroccan tea glasses, only they are finer and not decorated in the same way), which usually come in colored glass and are perfect for many roles: nightlights on the table, champagne (which is my favorite—they are the perfect receptacle for those gentle party bubbles), eau de vie or the perfect little machiatto, and even flowers.

When you are out looking at antique glass try to neutralize your eye; if you see something that you like,

LOOK OUT FOR MINI-HIGHBALLS (THEY ARE LIKE MOROCCAN TEA GLASSES, ONLY THEY ARE FINER AND NOT DECORATED IN THE SAME WAY), WHICH USUALLY COME IN COLORED GLASS AND ARE PERFECT FOR MANY ROLES.

look at it as a beautiful object rather than, say, a tumbler. This will make it much easier for you to find good uses for it. Instead of seeing the tumbler, for example, you can start to see a vase or a jar for heavy cream. A lot of the old shapes have very wide rims, which makes them useful for many things other than liquid. Glasses don't even have to be very old or ornate. One of my most useful and loved glasses is a Guinness pint glass that someone left at my house. It is used more than any other thing. Sadly the gold is wearing off now, but I have had flowers in it, long biscotti with coffee and my morning latte comes in it every day.

Unless you drink shots I would avoid buying those glasses altogether, or at least don't buy too many as they have few uses. There are a lot of small straight-sided tumblers around that are really tiny, like two inches high. It took me a long time to work out what to do with them and I bought them before I knew, just because they were so pretty. One now has Q-tips in it, which looks so lovely, and another often contains salt or something like that.

Straight-sided tiny tumblers are also lovely to use if anyone ever wants a slug of whiskey or vodka on the rocks. I don't get asked for either of these drinks very much and I must start offering them. It sounds so stylish, "on the rocks," doesn't it? All that jangling ice, it reminds me of *Dallas;* Sue Ellen spent a lot of her time on the rocks with one of those in her hand.

While you are trudging around looking at old bits of glass, think of bathrooms. If you come across a vase of the right shape, it can be perfect for cotton balls, which I always find rather a bore left in the plastic bag because they just always fall over.

Watch out for . . .

When you are buying glass there are things that you must look out for, like cloudiness, in which case don't even bother with it. Sometimes it is deeply tempting when the item in question is divinely pretty and the price is basement low, but it will cost you a fortune to get the cloudiness out, as it has to be put in an acid bath. I am not sure why it costs so much, but it does. In fact, cloudy glasses are so undesirable that you should keep an eye out for dodgy dealers who rub oil on the inside of their damaged glass so you buy it unawares. A friend of mine who is a very canny dealer and has been in the trade for years fell into this trap, and she was buying from someone whom she knew.

When glass gets a nick in it around the rim, it can be filed down quite easily. This is worth remembering both when you have something at home you don't want to throw away and when you are out shopping. For this reason, check the rims of glasses that you take a shine to; sometimes when they are filed down, if they are done badly, you get a very sharp edge, which is not very comfortable on the lips.

You also don't want to pay the price as though it

were perfect, which means that you may end up having to leave it, as you can't always expect to get a dealer down enough on things like that. He will have bought it for a certain price and will not want to sell it for any less.

BED LINEN

Flea markets and antique fairs are some of the best places to buy linen. If you buy antique sheets, they are deliciously soft and about a tenth of the price that they are when new. For a successful trip, ensure you go armed with the measurements of your bed. If your bed is four feet six inches, digging around markets is fantastically easy, but larger than that and it becomes slightly harder. It seems that people used to sleep very cosily in tiny beds. You also need to look out for wear and potential tear as the best night you have in linen sheets will be the night before you put your foot through them (see "Watch out for," opposite).

On your forays around the markets, it is much easier to find pillowcases, but they basically come in only two sizes. You will also find a lot of single pillowcases, which is a slight bore because invariably you will want pairs. But don't despair if you see a single one that you love; very often you can find something else in the pile that doesn't match but will work with it. While I have a horror of mismatched sheets, it doesn't seem to matter when you have bought things to work together. If they are all white and antique, this is coordination enough.

Old quilts and blankets are the fun things for the bed, because it is with these that you really start to change the look of a bedroom. They can be extremely expensive, however, depending on where you are looking, but most of the old quilts have two sides that you can use. This is not only great for getting two looks for the price of one, but they look so pretty when you turn them back to reveal the underside. This, in fact, is what they were designed for, as usually one pattern is quite large and strong while the other is smaller, which makes it feel more like a lining fabric.

When using quilts, I find it much prettier either to fold them along the end of the bed or to cover the bed as far as the pillows. I don't like pillows under the quilt; it looks very heavy. You are inevitably going to fall in love with a quilt that is for the wrong size of bed. This is most upsetting but I have never let it hold me back as you can still use them on double beds—you just have to put them across the end of the bed rather than have it cover it completely, which from an aesthetic point of view is absolutely fine.

Watch out for . . .

When buying linen, you must unfold the sheets—don't panic about the horrible stares coming at you from the proprietor—and hold them up to the light. You can then see very easily where the sheets have worn thin or even been darned. I wouldn't bother buying darned sheets unless it is around the edges, because they are not very comfortable—and certainly leave any that are too thin in places, because they are going to rip before too long.

When the sheets do rip don't throw them out. My grandmother used to have them turned into pillowcases, which is fabulous if you are so inclined to get handy with your sewing machine or know someone who can. I personally just rip them up into rags as they are excellent for drying glass because they are so soft and they don't leave behind any lint. You will need to make them larger than a normal dishcloth. Because the fabric is so much thinner than a normal one, it gets wet much more quickly so it needs to be doubled up.

STORAGE
SOLUTIONS

STORAGE
SOLUTIONS

Practical is one of my least favorite words. It always seemed to come out of my mother's mouth just as something I thought was great was about to be declared a no-go, like a truly magnificent pair of shoes that didn't quite fit or a deeply frivolous color. To my mind, practical things are always boring. But there are areas where a little practicality makes way for the good things in life. Like storage, for example, which successfully hides one's laundry. (How depressing are socks drying on the radiators? Extremely.) It is really worth building closets because although it is an expensive thing to do it will be the saving of your sanity.

Your bedroom will never be tidy unless you can put away your clothes, and hanging an old linen sheet in front of a hanging rail is not the answer. When you are looking at homes, either to buy or rent, it is really important to look at storage. Estate agents have this extraordinary idea about where one keeps one's stuff; they seem to place very little importance on closets. I was once shown a flat that had the most beautiful sitting room that was twenty feet square with amazingly high ceilings and a bank of French windows across one side. The bedroom, on the other hand, had been created out of what had been the landing before the house had been carved up by really second-rate developers (which sadly most of them are). The bed took up the whole width of the room, to the point where you couldn't open the shutters, and there was certainly no room to house a sock, much less my clothes.

When I brought this up, the estate agent suggested I get some storage boxes or build closets in the sitting room. I didn't buy the flat. It was kind of heartbreaking and I did think about it, but you cannot live like that. My mum was standing close by with her "it just isn't practical" lines, but the thing is, like mums so often are, she was right and I kept on looking. Your home can never be tidy if there isn't enough space to store the junk, and that will eventually drive you crazy.

Your home can never be tidy if there isn't enough space to store the junk, and that will eventually drive you crazy.

BEDROOM CLOSETS

You can buy old armoires, which are beautiful, but they tend not to have a huge amount of space, so whether or not they are suitable largely depends on how much clothes you have. I find they are generally better for men. Old linen presses are lovely, too (they are those antique cupboards that have cupboard doors above with shelves inside and drawers below), and they become yet more practical if you remove the shelves and replace them with a hanging rail. If you do this, remember not to throw away the shelves. Should you ever want to resell the press, you will devalue it by not having them. Unless it is a very good piece of furniture, don't worry too much about putting in a hanging rail. Its value in your life will be greatly increased by one, which will far outweigh any other consideration.

You can also find antique wardrobes that were built as such and these can be very beautiful. The major benefit of antique wardrobes is that you can spend less on them than built-in closets and you can take them with you when you move. But, again, you don't always get as much space as you do if you build closets, or the space might not be divided in quite the right way.

Built-in closets

If you are going to build closets you must sit down and think quite carefully about what you have to keep in there. Because they are expensive to make, they have got to be worth it. Try to make sure they are divided, as so often you look into closets and there is just one rod going from one end of it to the other, which can be really unsatisfactory. Think about what you want to include in your closet—long clothes, folded clothes, shoes—and then think of how best to store them.

Do not allow your contractors to get away with giving you cheap drawers; if your budget can't take in drawers, then have shelves. Bad drawers will break eventually, which is just a nightmare, the king of false economies. Look at how many long coats you need to hang, any long dresses or even long skirts. Can you fit double hanging or is it best to have single hanging with drawers/shelves underneath?

Space is usually quite precious, so be clever with it. You do need to give your clothes space, because if they are packed into a small space on metal hangers they will look awful very quickly. I have made one of my closets with single hanging and two deep drawers at the bottom, which have turned out to be fantastically useful. First they had my suitcases in them and now they house all my wrapping papers and ribbons and treasures. They were actually an accident as I had planned for them to be a really brilliant form of shoe storage, which in reality did not work one bit. But as it turns out they are fabulous as they have solved the problem of that void, the black hole that is the bottom of the closet, home to broken shoes.

Hang-ups

It is of the utmost importance to make sure your clothes sit on good hangers. They need to be padded, as wire and thin plastic hangers, while being free from the dry cleaners and clothes shops, will wreck your clothes. Now, such purchases cost more than people are generally prepared to spend, so it is probably worth thinking of the hanger in terms of the outfit you are going to put on it. Jackets and coats that have been on wire coat hangers just look awful, as they lose their shoulders.

If you are in the 99.9999 percent of the population who would not consider themselves wealthy enough to equip their closets with smart hangers, think again. The only reason you think that is because it is a boring thing to spend money on and the idea of walking into a shop and getting enough for all your clothes is quite scary. So do it this way. The next time you buy something that breaks a new budget barrier, go and buy a decent hanger to hang it on. The cost of the hanger will seem like a small cost compared to the item and you can put it down to upkeep. Just continue doing this and slowly infiltrate them into your wardrobe. You do have to watch padded hangers slightly because they are like teaspoons: somehow they walk. Even when you live alone they have an extraordinary way of disappearing.

YOU DO HAVE TO WATCH PADDED HANGERS SLIGHTLY BECAUSE THEY ARE LIKE TEASPOONS: SOMEHOW THEY WALK.

The top of the closet

This is the perfect place for winter clothes and suitcases and you probably don't need me to tell you that, as I am sure that is pretty universal. What is quite a handy tip is the zip-up plastic storage bags that you can get. It is too depressing to put all those sweaters away for the summer (I know it is unlikely) and when you come back to them in the autumn there has been the moth equivalent of a busman's holiday going on in the merino. To avoid this, wash everything before putting it into the plastic zip-up bags and then put the nozzle of the vacuum in the opening and suck all the air out of the bag—vacuum packed. This will prevent the moths and it will also give you a lot more space—think of all that bulky skiwear that can be reduced by sucking the life out of it. In fact, it would be a really cool thing to do with your packing; just make sure you do it only when you are going to places where you will be able to do the same on the return trip, or you may find you have trouble getting it all back in.

YOU CAN'T REASON WITH AN INSECT AND BY THE TIME THEY ARE THAT FAT AND GROSS THEY AREN'T EATING YOUR SWEATERS ANY LONGER; IT IS STRANGE, BUT THEY ONLY FEAST WHEN THEY ARE SO SMALL YOU CAN'T SEE THEM, DEVIOUS LITTLE WRETCHES.

The moth

It is a good thing to keep lavender bags or camphor bricks in your closets as they will ward off moths and leave everything smelling delicious. It is a beautiful idea to put loose lavender stems between the sheets and it does look great for a photo shoot, but in reality it gets everywhere and makes everything a bit dusty. Try to remember to change lavender bags as they loose their smell. This should be done once a year.

There is another trick for moths and that is horse chestnuts, which my friend Cindy swears by. She has all her drawers lined with them—and no moths. The real bonus of these is that they don't smell—well not to us; they obviously smell appalling if you are a moth—but not everyone is dead keen on smelling of either lavender or camphor. Horse chestnuts benefit from being incredibly easy to find and don't cost a thing, and they are a lot more practical than one of my early moth-repellent ideas, which came about when I saw a very large and heavy moth that had clearly been living on a diet of the purest cashmere. It was struggling across my sitting room in the direction of my bedroom so, furious, I leaped up and killed it with my shoe against the sitting room door. Not sure what to do next, I left it there, to Rowan's horror, who asked what on earth I was doing. So I told him I was planning to leave it there as a warning to other cashmere munchers on their way to the land of silk and merino: my bedroom.

Of course, it doesn't work. You can't reason with an insect and by the time they are that fat and gross they aren't eating your sweaters any longer; it is strange, but they only feast when they are so small you can't see them, devious little wretches.

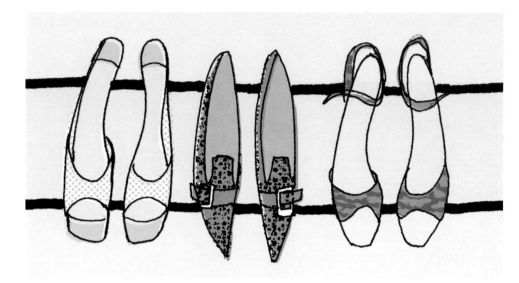

SHOES

Then there are the shoes. How often are they left kicking around the bottom of the closet? It is amazing how they can get so neglected when a new pair of shoes is just so exciting and usually rather naughty. Don't you always promise yourself that you will keep them looking like new forever? Then, with the first scuff, they start their slide down that slippery slope that is our affections until eventually they go from being our most favorite party shoes to every-day-with-jeans shoes. I quite like that look, though—the battered party shoe—they are a bit like strung-out junkies who were once great beauties but who saw too many late nights.

To avoid this happening, build shelves in the bottom of your closets for your shoes, like steps, or you can put the brass rods in. Make sure you keep the rods close enough together so your shoes don't slip in between them. There is another thing that a lot of fashionistas do; they

THE HIGHER THE BED, THE LESS VISUAL SPACE IT TAKES UP IN THE ROOM AND YOU ARE LEFT WITH PLENTY OF ROOM TO STORE THINGS UNDERNEATH.

Polaroid their shoes and stick the picture on the front of the shoe box. While I have admired this greatly I have never got into it myself as I tend to find I am not very good at getting things back into the right boxes the whole time. (I also think it looks rather a mess because the boxes get very scrappy with all that opening and closing and the Polaroids are never very good.)

Alternatively, buy storage boxes in either frosted or clear plastic that are the same size as a shoe box. They are good to use as you can see the shoe. It is not a bad idea to keep shoes in boxes because they do get awfully dusty if they are left out. I keep my shoes in front of the fireplace in my bedroom, which I love as I love looking at them, but they do need a bit of a dust every now and then. A friend of my mum's, who is a superstylish "old-school" American gentleman artist, keeps his shoes all around the baseboards of his bedroom and dressing room. They look fabulous as they are all beautiful handmade English shoes with wooden shoe trees in them, immaculately polished. There is something about old gentlemen and their shoes that is just so reassuring.

Shoes need categorizing with the closets—you would never really keep your wellies near your party shoes, would you? So keep outdoor footwear at the bottom of the closet with the outdoor clothes. Likewise, you simply cannot have your Polartek next to the silk; the outdoor stuff will make the evening things smell (they do all have very different scents). While your ball dress might smell of a combination of Guerlain and cigars, outdoor coats will definitely smell of mud, sweat and dogs and they should never cross-odorize.

If you have a house, usually all that sort of muddy stuff remains somewhere near a door, but when you live in a flat it is slightly harder to find a space for them. I so rarely use my outside boots that they are kept in a tied-up plastic bag in the top of my closet and I keep forgetting they are there. It is quite a good idea to leave them behind sometimes. The times I have been most successful in avoiding country walks is when I arrive with a couple of pairs of high heels and some wildly impractical pair of suede shoes for the daytime.

Clever extra bedroom storage

This has become extremely fashionable of late and there are many, many shops selling all sorts of boxes and cloth-covered things that look like Victorian beach tents. But most of it is not terribly desirable. You can keep a multitude of junk under your bed. Not the usual old shoes kicked under there by accident six months ago, but organized junk, properly packaged. If you are moving into a new home and happen to be buying a new bed at the same time, it is worth considering the amount of storage space you have compared to what you need. If there is not a lot of room for closets in your bedroom, which is more than likely, you need to find alternatives. Buy a bed that gives you height; the higher the bed, the less visual space it takes up in the room and you are left with plenty of room to store things underneath. This is the joy of old brass beds. You can keep a lot of things that don't need to be accessed too often in sealed plastic boxes.

Double a chest of drawers as a bedside table, but you will need to watch the height. You don't want it to come too far above your head when you are lying down, but you can get low chests of drawers and you can get high beds. This works particularly well in guest bedrooms where you don't usually have enough room for much, and it will save you a piece of furniture, too.

Guest bedrooms

It is extremely tempting to use a guest bedroom and its closets for all those clothes you can't quite bear to chuck out. Try not to, for as a guest it is not that salubrious to sleep in someone's dumping ground and in the end you won't really enjoy it. If your guest bedroom is of the small variety pay heed to what I did for a client whose room was really quite small. Once I had failed to persuade him to knock it out and make his bathroom much bigger, we went about making it into a lovely and cozy bedroom that would be comfortable for his mother and friends but not so great that anyone would think of staying for longer than a couple of nights. Most of the room was taken up with a bed, which left little to no room for a closet. This is where I first used a small chest of drawers as a bedside table. It was mirrored, which looked very elegant, and was not too heavy, and then for hanging I found a panel of old hooks in an antique shop, which we hung on the wall behind the door with hangers covered in fabric that worked in the room. You must offer hanging space for guests or their

> Don't throw away worn-out sheets; they make fabulous dishcloths. Because they are so soft from years of being washed they will not leave any lint on clean glass and get a shine up like nothing else.

room is just going to be so chaotic for the duration of their stay. The panel of hooks trick is such a good way of not spending a fortune on closets in a room that you barely use, even if you do have the space.

If you are able to have a bathroom that is en suite with a guest bedroom and the bedroom really is small, then you can always provide storage in the bathroom. It is almost better to have a larger bathroom and then a tiny bedroom that is all bed. Once you have no mess in the bedroom, like clothes and stuff, it is rather glamorous to have a bath/dressing room. It is really a question of allocating space to your best advantage. Having an en suite bathroom also means that you can keep all the sheets and towels for that room in the top of a bathroom cabinet, which will come out as the guests arrive, making space for their things. Trunks (proper old ones from the days when men didn't complain about how much luggage girls had on fabulous old liners) at the ends of beds are not only decorative (sorry, a ghastly word, which makes one think of ornamental cabbages and hideous painted furniture) but they hide a fantastic amount of things that you don't want to be

completely rid of or even blankets and eiderdowns when they are not being used. Piles of old suitcases make very good bedside tables and they have the added bonus of you being able to pick them up in flea markets for not very much money.

Organizing and keeping linen

The first thing to do is to work out what not to keep, like your child's *Star Wars* duvet cover long after he has left university. Remember to chuck out, give away or send down to the local charity shop with some regularity (but do check what charities your local shop supports; I got a rude shock the other day when I stumbled across an anti-Nazi demonstration going on outside a charity shop where I had dumped loads of old clothes). Don't throw away worn-out sheets; they make fabulous dishcloths. Because they are so soft from years of being washed they will not

leave any lint on clean glass and get a shine up like nothing else. Only bother doing this with either pure cotton or linen (be careful not to cut them too small, because the fabric is thinner than a normal tea towel so you will need more of it, or it just gets far too wet too quickly).

You may have sheets that you will want to hang on to that are neither worn-out nor have Luke Skywalker all over them but don't necessarily use very often and are relegated to the guest bed. Bundle up these sets and tie them together. It is a total nightmare trying to find matching sheets in the right sizes when they are all piled up together. Inevitably you are in a hurry when you are making up your guest bed, and if the sheets are not labeled, there is only one way to find out what size they are, and being left with a pile of unfolded sheets is really hellish. So put together sets and tie them up with legal tape.

Traditionally, linen used to be tied together with grosgrain ribbon, frightfully chic but no longer terribly practical, whereas legal tape is inexpensive and can be bought in the UK in stationery shops specializing in supplies for lawyers, and it comes in pink. Label the bundles with luggage labels—these come in the traditional brown or white but are also available in colors. Then you know what is what and will not be so frustrated by floating oddments in the closets (tie the labels with bows, not knots, or you will have to cut them and write new labels every time you use the sheets).

If you are short of closet space, then keep sheets and pillowcases in sealed boxes under the bed (it is quite amazing just how many boxes you can fit under a bed), but make sure the boxes seal properly, particularly if they are in a room that is rarely used, or you may fall foul of a few moths (see page 227 for anti-moth remedies).

BATHROOMS

As you may have gathered by now, as far as I am concerned, bathrooms are simply incomplete without an awful lot of oils and scrubs. These all take up quantities of space and you need to have them within easy reach during your bath. There are a couple of routes to make this as simple as possible. For example, I am now going in for the built-in bath, and with this you gain a lot of space around the side if you make it deep enough, but it isn't usually enough.

If you are redoing your bathroom from scratch you are bound to have pipes that run along the side of a wall. These will then need to be boxed in and the rest of the wall plasterboarded so it is flush with the boxed-in pipes. Then there comes the bit where you get a shelf. Have your contractor cut out a void the depth of the boxed-in pipes and high enough to take the bottles of oils and then tile it in with the rest of the walls. This is the single most useful thing I have done in bathrooms and it looks great, too.

If you are not going to be doing much work to the bathroom and don't have the space to do this, then put up glass shelves either beside or at one end of the bath. You can buy those metal soap dish racks that attach to the wall and hang over the bath. In the same line you will probably find a longer one for sponges, which works very well for a few bottles when you are short of space.

Towels are another thing you may find you need to keep in the bathroom, particularly if you don't have much storage space elsewhere. I have found that old luggage racks are perfect to put up on the wall quite high. There are few things in life more pleasing than piles of clean towels; it is very spalike, which is precisely what your bathroom should be. Personally I find shelves in bathrooms a lot more appealing than cabinets, as you lose stuff in there—years of old makeup and face creams. Generally all these things are good to look at, so keep them out and within easy reach.

For the things that you don't want on display use boxes—beside the toilet have a jar for all your tampons (there are some things that need to be kept slightly hidden but within easy reach). It is easy to find lovely boxes for all the other goodies that men don't need to know about but that girls must have close by. Keep the toilet paper in abundance beside the toilet, too—I like using a basket piled high. My godmother has old washbasins (also easy to find in flea markets; they are the bowls that used to have jugs in them, but more often than not you find them without their jugs) with a few rolls in them. Having a lot of toilet paper out is reassuring as there is nothing worse than being caught short and it means you don't have to store it somewhere else.

UTILITY CLOSETS

We all have a different amount of space for utility or laundry rooms or closets, and it is worth finding a space for it all when you first move into a place. In my first home I had a washer-dryer in the kitchen. There was simply no extra space for it anywhere else, and a lot of the drying ended up on the radiators in the sitting room, like dead voles hanging on a country fence, which is a bit depressing. When I moved, one of the first things I looked for was how I could create a separate space for the machines and all the hullabaloo that goes with them.

There are about three different space scenarios I would imagine, the first being no space, the second being room for a closet and the third is a room dedicated to the chores. If you can possibly help it, try to avoid having the machines in either your kitchen or your bathroom unless these rooms are a decent size. The kitchen is probably the better of the two, but it depends on the space and layout of your home and life. If you can build a closet for all of this, then that is great. Put your machines side by side with a counter over the top. Formica (which I would say most of the time is horrible) is perfect here and it comes in about fifty colors, so choose your favorite. Then paint the inside of the closet something delightful that pleases your eye; after all, a little prettiness in the laundry closet lessens the dread of having to open that door.

If you are tall it is wise to consider carefully the height of your counter (this also applies to your kitchen counter), as raising it above the standard height will save your back from all that bending over; consider filling the void between the machines and the counter with drawers.

Keep everything in baskets on your counter waiting to be washed, dried or ironed. All your laundry products can be kept there too, and then above that you can have shelves for the bed linen and towels. Have a small mezzanine-style shelf for the household tools that you need below the linen. The standard-size depth of a washing machine is about sixteen inches so that will dictate the size of your counter and give you something to work with when you are looking for the space in which to put this closet. The mezzanine shelf should be quite shallow. It is such a bore to have deep shelves because you can never get to the stuff at the back so I would make it about the depth of a shoe box and remember to have it high enough above the counter for you to fit a large box of detergent underneath. Then the shelves above need to be just deep enough for the sheets and towels.

It is a good idea to have quite a few of these shelves as it is best not to pile things too high and it makes

Paint the inside of a closet something delightful that pleases your eye; after all, a little prettiness in the laundry closet lessens the dread of having to open that door.

it easier to keep the closets tidy. The less you pull from the bottom of a large pile, the less it all collapses and you can never really be bothered to put it all back neatly when you are in the middle of changing the beds.

The great thing about this space is that you can hide a multitude of mess in it. You know how it is when it is 8:15 P.M. and someone like your picky mother-in-law is coming to dinner (aka to check the house over)? I have regularly found myself tossing piles of the week's worn clothes in there, old shopping bags and anything else that I have found on my bedroom floor. This is a far superior hiding place to under the bed, as you will always forget about the things you have kicked there in that moment of panic and self-loathing at such studenty behavior. With this beautiful laundry, however, it won't be long before you open its doors and have to deal with the consequences of your hurried housework.

The housemaid's cupboard

I love this term. My mother introduced me to it when I moved into my first flat; she opened a closet door and announced it would be the housemaid's cupboard. I had no idea what she was talking about and she looked at me as though I had told her I wasn't sure what a dictionary was and explained that it was for the housemaid's mop and overalls and stuff. Actually, it wasn't quite that bad but more thrillingly I was able to announce back that, in fact, the closet was already allocated to Rowan and his clothes. I do now have a housemaid's cupboard, even though it is sadly me that flings the feather duster around the tops of the pictures, and cannot imagine life without one. I really am not at all sure where the vacuum or the ironing board lived in my former dwelling.

So housemaid or not, you need to make a tall and skinny closet to house the ironing board, brooms and vacuum. It is very easy to forget about these tall and cumbersome objects and where you are going to put them. Fortunately, there are some handy ways to keep the ironing board from behaving like a deck chair; with a large hook on the back wall you can usually hang it up. Brooms can be hung up as well with a pair of nails spaced a little less far apart than the width of the brush end of the broom; then just hang it upside down. I find that vacuum cleaners benefit from having the long metal tube removed from that snake that goes into the main part of the machine; otherwise there is just far too much tubing for a normal person to have to deal with.

KITCHEN STORAGE

The hell of saucepans in cupboards—it always sounds as though someone is being killed when you have to pull one from the back. If I had the space I would have them all hanging from the ceiling on those metal hooks over one of the work surfaces. But I don't so I have to struggle with them in a corner cupboard. They are a lot easier to cope with if you stack them with the lids on upside down. For me, open shelving is the smartest. I love being able to see all my glasses and plates and they become so much easier to get at and, more important, to put away (I just forget about anything that is in a cupboard; I am a very out-of-sight-out-of-mind person). That may be why there are eight packets of sugar in my kitchen cabinet and nothing remotely useful like something to have for dinner. The open shelves are only really useful for things you use regularly or else they are going to get very dusty and greasy if you are a keen cook.

I like as much out as possible and this goes for all the cleaning products as well—dishwasher tablets are my favorite because they have the nicest wrappers. Let's face it, they all wash the dishes so for me the wrapper is the best way to find the product I would prefer to use. I keep them in a vase above the dishwasher and chuckle whenever I watch my friends momentarily reach for one, thinking they are sweets. I suggested this in *Vogue* once but some do-gooder called in to complain. She thought I was terribly irresponsible as one of her little darlings might eat one. I consulted with my mother, the voice of all reason, and then felt a whole lot better as she sensibly pointed out that no child would eat very much of a dishwasher tablet because they taste revolting. I remember always trying to eat bouillon cubes and I couldn't understand how something that came in such a lovely wrapper could taste so horrible. I thought that if I persevered they might get better. I was not the most intelligent of children, and eventually I asked what they were and realized they were never going to taste good.

Dishwashing liquid is improved if it is decanted into a lovely bottle with one of those olive oil drizzle stoppers pushed in the top. I like keeping all the brushes and sponges in an old china kitchen jar. Mine says Moist Sugar and you can find them in most antique shops that deal in kitchenware and even modern kitchen shops will have something. Don't use glass because the bottom will get nasty and marked from the dripping water and will never look pretty.

For all those rolls of stuff like waxed paper, foil, plastic wrap and paper towels, I think having them sticking out the top of another vase is good. I have a glazed pottery one, which I love, and it just means that they are always close at hand, and every time you don't have to open a

DISHWASHING LIQUID IS IMPROVED IF IT IS DECANTED INTO A LOVELY BOTTLE WITH ONE OF THOSE OLIVE OIL DRIZZLE STOPPERS PUSHED IN THE TOP.

drawer or cupboard, you don't have to close it either, which really does help with keeping everything tidy.

Drawers are always better than cabinets for pots, pans and large plates or dishes. Stacking is a bad idea because getting things out from the bottom of the pile is just too much like hard work. When you are building a kitchen, drawers will be more expensive than cabinets and you want to get really good ones or they will break. Personally I would lose the waste disposal before I got rid of the drawers, but then I have never actually had one of those as an option; my kitchens have always been built on the tightest of budgets. I have never had drawers either, but I would like to.

China and glass

How you store this depends entirely on how much you have and how much space you have. As I have said, all mine is on two open shelves in my kitchen and anything that couldn't fit is in a cabinet where it sits quietly forgotten. So this is my personal preference, but then I don't have kitchen china and formal china. If you have a lot, which is very easy to end up with, you will need to build cupboards for it all. If you don't store it properly it is going to get chipped, which is heartbreaking. I would always recommend shallow shelving so you only fit one size of plate on one shelf, rather than stack them too high. You should also cover the shelves in baize; this does not have to be dark green as any felt will do and it comes in just about a zillion great colors, so go crazy.

I am afraid I can't tell you the measurements that you are going to need with which to space out your shelves. You are going to have to sit down and work out what you have and actually measure it, remembering to leave a couple of inches of space at the top so that it is not too tight. If you are short of space, these cupboards don't have to be in the kitchen; it is pretty handy to have them in your dining room or dining area. I once made someone cabinets to keep all of this in. At the top were drawers for his silver and then underneath a combination of drawers and shelves for the china, all lined in baize. If you have silver cutlery this is advisable because it prevents it from tarnishing.

Keep your glasses upside down as it stops them from getting dusty. Keep them in order of size and color, too. It is one of the most beautiful things: rows and rows of clean glass, and one of the least appealing when you see a haphazard collection of dusty glasses. It is so much easier to find the right number of the size that you want if they are kept in an orderly fashion. I used to spend hours organizing my mum's glass cupboard—sad, I know, but there it is. If you are building cupboards for the china, do the same for the glass and have them on baize too; it will prevent chipping. Otherwise have them out on more open shelving; they are a delight for the eye.

IT IS ONE OF THE MOST
BEAUTIFUL THINGS: ROWS
AND ROWS OF CLEAN GLASS.
I USED TO SPEND HOURS
ORGANIZING MY MUM'S GLASS
CUPBOARD—SAD, I KNOW,
BUT THERE IT IS.

DOMESTIC CHORES

DOMESTIC CHORES

In my life, there is this imaginary area somewhere about a few feet above the right side of my head. It is just beyond the distance of my outstretched arm and it is where all the hideous things that I don't want to do are filed. The strange thing is that before they end up there, they are quite easy tasks, so to stop menial tasks from becoming hideous, you must strike while the iron is hot. Like all things that you don't want to do, they carry enormous satisfaction value once they have been done. Among these tasks lie the Domestic Chores, but fortunately there are ways to add a little glamour to them and ways to make them a little easier. A lot of it is attitude, and the rest is making sure that the end result is quite delicious, like making your bed beautifully. If you make it badly, it has still been a bore to make and it will not be very satisfying to get into. After a good two hours of domesticating, I do feel how I imagine people feel when they get back from the gym. But I'll tell you something: it's a lot more gratifying. After all, when you get back from working out, what have you got? A bag full of laundry.

Almost all the time, the things in life that are hard to do are the ones we don't have a handle on, like dealing with the bank manager. But if you are organized and you know what is going on with him, he is not so scary to call. It is exactly the same with the chores. If you have everything for the housework in good order and well stocked, then it is just so much easier and rewarding to do. Usually the closet with the vacuum and stuff is just a mess and you run the risk of killing yourself every time you open the door because everything is jammed in, pressed against the door, waiting to fall out as soon as you open it. So make sure everything fits easily into your Housemaid's Cupboard and the same goes for the utility closet. Mostly you are doing bits and pieces around the house before or after work or on the weekends and it makes the jobs so much more difficult if you don't have everything right there. There is also something weirdly satisfying about setting up your closets and cabinets with all the right stuff.

It is worth initiating a self-reward scheme that goes with a good couple of hours of housework. For example, keep some treats in the laundry closet, in the shape of a box of violet creams perhaps. I quite like to do a home pedicure before the vacuuming, so that in my mind I am simply vacuuming to pass the time needed for my nails to dry; a facemask would have the same effect. A cappuccino and a gossip is a reward that would get me very busy with the duster.

THE GENERAL WHIP ROUND THE HOUSE

Coming home at night to a mess is deeply depressing, but it is one of those things that however much the angel side of your brain tells you to tidy your sitting room before you go to bed, make your bed every day before you leave for work and make sure the dishes are done as you go, there is that lazy little devil on the other side saying, "Oh, leave it, you can do it later." Don't panic, it is only the dreariest of people who have everything immaculate all the time. There are some shortcuts to make it all look less dreadful, like plumping up the cushions on the sofas. This is not hard work; do it quickly before you go to bed or to work in the

A cappuccino and a gossip is a reward that would get me very busy with the duster.

morning and the room will look 80 percent better in a flash. If you don't have time to make your bed before you leave, pull it back and have the duvet or the blankets folded along the end of the bed with the pillows. Suddenly it looks as though you are airing the bed rather than just being a slob.

I usually save the housework for Saturday mornings. Don't get dressed; do the housework in your underwear. It is much easier and boys love it, especially if you are in your best high heels. From a more practical point of view, flinging yourself around the place with vacuums and dusters is a hot business. I also find that some good music playing—as loud as possible—really helps with getting the work done, because if you can successfully sidetrack your mind into singing and dancing, you will hardly notice the chores.

The order of events

I am not especially ordered about how I clean. There will be times when the bed has been completely stripped and the vacuum is out, the new sheets on the floor and the bathroom is halfway through being blitzed. This does not matter; you will find the way that you work best and it just so happens that chaos is the atmosphere that works best for me. Open all the windows before you start, or if it is cold outside, wait until you have warmed up, which won't take long. It is very important to air the rooms as they can get quite stuffy and also the cleaning products that you use stink, especially in the bathroom. I wouldn't bother going in for any of that spring-meadow-scented nonsense, or any of those revolting things that you spray on your sofa to get rid of the smell of dogs and cigarettes; that is not getting anything clean at all.

Start your rou-
tine with the
sheets on your
bed, which must
be changed once a week.
You presumably want your
bed to be crisp and delicious at
all times. I find it astonishing that boys
don't think this is deeply important too,
when one of their priorities is to get girls into
their beds. What do they think changing their
sheets once a month is doing for their cause?

Now for the dust. This is my real bugbear, for
almost as soon as you have got rid of it, it appears
again. You really want to be careful how you tackle it,
as you can find yourself just moving it around the room.
You need damp cloths or these new wipes that lift the dust
and keep it clinging to the cloth. There is hardly any point
in doing it any other way and you need to do this at least
once a week. But the dust for me has different areas of importance. There are the obvious ones like all the tables and
surfaces, and then there are the hidden ones that you forget about until you start to move any furniture, which is
when you get a real shock. The tops of pictures, the windowsills, the baseboards, the bookshelves and the tops of
lampshades and lightbulbs also fall into this category. (Did
you know that you can lose half the light from a dirty
lightbulb? I just dust them with a duster, but you can remove and wash them in warm, soapy water if you are
more thorough than I am. Just make sure you don't wet
the metal part, and dry them properly before putting them
back in the lamp.) This extra level of dusting does not
need to be done once a week. Instead, about once a month

do a really good once-over, or do one of the things every week so you spread the work.

Treats to get you around the house with the duster

- Don't start the cleaning without doing your toenails, a masque or a twenty-minute intense hair-conditioning treatment first. Any or all of these things will give you a reason to do something as dull as housework, because they all need time either to dry or work.
- Play good music for dusting, vacuuming or laundry. Listen to any talk radio station for the ironing.
- Plan a lunch date at the end of it; you don't really need to do more than a few hours and a deadline really gets you going.
- Make sure you have coffee and a cookie. This is a treat in itself and one you can only really have when you are at home in the daytime. So break from the cleaning for a cappuccino and a biscuit or two.
- Hide some treats in the laundry closet, something you will forget about until you are doing the wash. It is good to reward yourself for such boring tasks.
- Run yourself a spoilingly hot and heavily scented bath at the end of your hours of cleaning. It serves a double purpose: it gives you a well-deserved soak and it will eradicate the horrid smells of those cleaning products from your bathroom.
- Scented candles are definitely a good thing to light at the end of a cleaning session so you can sit back and enjoy your clean and delicious smelling home.
- Remember to buy the papers or the new issues of your favorite magazines so you can look forward to an afternoon lazing around the house going through them.

UTILITY CUPBOARD

Utility closets incorporating a washing machine and dryer are a great alternative when you don't have the space to have a room taken over by laundry (see the section on utility closets in "Storage Solutions," page 236, for more on practical details). It is such a shame to allow the really interminably dull areas of life to get their own way and remain uninspiring drudges. Amazingly, the utility closet is a space that can become great rather than hideous.

If you keep it filled with lovely things and looking vaguely pretty, it is going to become a far less gruesome door to open and you will find the rest of your house benefits as a result. For example, keep a huge supply of vacuum cleaner bags—I mean, who wants to have to shop for those more than once a year? Also, make sure you have all the lightbulbs that you use in the house in good supply. I know this sounds really silly but when a lightbulb goes, it is the remembering to buy bulbs that is the reason you live in semidarkness for eight weeks. If you can smugly go off to your utility closet as soon as the bulb blows, it never becomes a chore.

You will need some toolboxes. These aren't necessarily only for screwdrivers and picture hooks, but for anything that you might need. Make sure you always have Scotch tape and scissors, a ball of string, extra plugs and a good supply of batteries. Superglue is always good to have, as without a few supplies you become grounded as soon as something goes wrong or breaks in the house.

It is amazing how quickly you learn to change a plug when you really have to. When I moved into my first home all the lamps had the wrong plugs for the sockets, so I realized that I was going to have to call the electrician to come and sort them all out. I had just about got as far as

> I have always found not to be able to do something immediately is one of the most frustrating things in life, and why is it that one only ever tries to fix things after the shops have all closed?

thinking what a ridiculous expense this is going to be when I became tired of waiting and I just started taking all the plugs off other things that I didn't need so badly or were broken and putting them, copycat fashion, onto the lamps. For this sort of work a packet of screwdrivers came in dead handy. The best ones to get are the little packs with six different heads and one handle because in that way you don't loose the heads. When I was a child I remember that the toolbox always had a pretty scanty collection of bits in it and it certainly never had the screwdriver in the size you needed. I have always found not to be able to do something immediately is one of the most frustrating things in life, and why is it that one only ever tries to fix things after the shops have all closed? It is never as though you can pop out and get the right tools, you have to wait, uuuuurrhg. That is why it is so important to have it all right there in the closet.

Tools and household bits and pieces

It is such fun putting boxes of things together. I am not sure what it is about having a shelf of old shoe boxes filled with useful things, but I love it. It is a bit like having boxes of treasures when you were little, and didn't you love filling your pencil case with really good pens and sharpeners and smelly erasers and things? From a styling point of view, you can get quite particular about these boxes. For example, you can get hold of clear plastic shoe boxes for storage, which are smart, or you can use old shoe/boot or bag boxes. (Again, the smart ones, naturally!)

There are times when it is fabulous to have everything new and shiny, but this is not one of them. For the toolboxes it is much better when everything is a bit old and well used. For example, the rags should be rags and not immaculately clean dish towels and the nails in the old jam jars should be a collection of old and new, some even maybe with a bit of plaster on them. If you don't have much use for nails and screws, which I must say I don't, then just keep a few in those little tiny jam jars you get in hotels and on airplanes (of course, you will have more use for them once you get an electric drill, which you must get). Always keep an eye out for screw-lid jars, particularly the ones that are good shapes, as it is amazing just how handy they are around the house, and when you go away somewhere they are good for taking detergent with you for your hand laundry.

Keep all your spare buttons in one jar and spools of thread in another, and then you can have yet another for all the safety pins and needles and a pair of scissors. I do find sewing baskets a bit of a pain. They are always a mess because the cotton threads are all in a knot, you can never find a needle until it is at least a quarter inch into your finger and somehow, however long ago you were at camp, there always seem to be a bunch of name tapes floating around the bottom. If you keep all your jars in boxes and label the lids, you will know at one glance which one holds the jar you need. Otherwise, just keep them on the shelf, sparkling clean. It is very important that you get all the labels and glue off, because otherwise they look really ugly and part of this whole ridiculous process is to make everything in your utility closet pretty and user-friendly. There is nothing very exciting about having to sew a button back onto a coat, but if it means going into the closet and using your beautiful jars filled with buttons and threads you can pretend for a bit that it is a pleasure. I probably sound totally whacked but it does work.

Proper workmen's tools

Power drills—they are my new number one accessory for girls. I have become obsessed with them and I can't think why I have not realized before that this is the final outpost of male superiority. I have got a rail that has been waiting to go up in my laundry closet for a year and a half since my ridiculous contractor trudged off without putting it up. My bathrobes have been hanging over my bathroom door because the hook is still sitting in the cupboard waiting for a passing man with a drill to put it up and now I have found a really wonderfully kitsch finger plate and a door handle for my bathroom door in a junk shop and refuse to wait any longer. It is not rocket science—drill, screws and wall—so why is this a task that we assume only men can do? Make sure you have a power drill in the closet and you will never again be infuriated waiting for these small tasks to be done. It is quite important to get some extra bits of equipment, too, like an electrical cable finder. The only thing worse than a bra burner is some dizzy girl doing her bit for women's rights and making us all look like idiots by short-circuiting the entire house.

THE LAUNDRY

The accessories you need to make this task more appealing are beautiful clothes pegs, deliciously spoiling scented waters for the iron and washing machine and special non-detergent organic hand wash for your sweaters. I have found a product, made in France by a Parisian florist called Hervé Gambs, which is concentrated scented water that you put in the fabric softener space in the washing machine and it leaves your washing smelling of jasmine, tuberose or orange blossom. There is just nothing very special about the smell of your more obvious fabric softeners; spring fresh or alpine meadow do not appeal to me very much. This is something that has bothered me for a while so I am thrilled with Hervé's blue glass bottles of deliciousness. I have also found that if I put a few drops of this in my water sprayer it scents the water, which is cheaper than buying bottles of lavender water for the iron.

Hand washing is just such a bore and it is so easy to pop everything in the machine, but be careful. Your underwear will eventually go gray. I am not sure why, but it just does and it will certainly lose its shape. Keep a few of those plastic basins in your bathroom, which will look less ghastly if you buy them in good colors. I have silver ones that are rather stylish; I would avoid the dark colors as it never feels very nice to be washing in murky water. Every night soak your panties and bras before you go to bed, then in the morning give them a quick wash, rinse them off and hang them out. But there is a shortcut: rinse in the machine (there should be a "delicates" option or "worn once" or something). Put the machine on that and don't put in any soap. I really like doing this because aside from it meaning I don't have to do it by hand, it feels like everything is being properly washed. I am not sure that I would recommend this with anything too lacy and delicate but it does halve your work.

Be careful with underwire bras, too, as their life span seems to shorten with all that spinning, and there are few things worse than that wire sticking into your chest halfway through the day. Tights must not go anywhere near either the machine or the dryer as they will snag, so hand wash those too. Wring them out properly, otherwise when you hang them to dry they will get longer and longer.

Wool needs special care and fortunately there is now that little wool sign on quite a lot of washing ma-

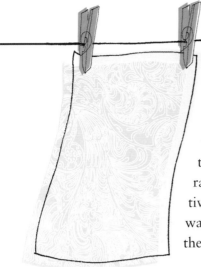

chines, which many people swear by. I used to as well until one of my sweaters came out fit for a pixie. I have never done it again. I just find that the first time you discover that washing machines work for wool you are frightfully careful and then as time goes on you find that you become rather blasé about it and are not quite so attentive with the dial. I recommend soaking in cold water with a wool washing liquid overnight and then rinsing and laying flat to dry.

Be careful when you are wringing out heavy knits as this is the moment they can stretch to oblivion. The water is so heavy that you should really wring it out before you lift them up. The best way to do this is to lay them flat in the bath or sink and roll them up from there. You can put them in the machine to spin, which will keep the shape better than when you wring out by hand.

Make sure there are loads of hooks in the airing cupboard; the more things you can hang over the boiler to dry, the better. Nail a brass rod to the wall over the bath so you can gently steam your clothes while you are running a bath. It is really important to keep clothes hanging out, but it is not necessarily a good thing to wash them or send them to the dry cleaners after every outing.

Don't panic, I am not suggesting that clothes should not be washed, but I do believe that some things can be hung in front of a window to take away the smell of cigarette smoke, which is distinctly preferable to spraying them with a product to mask the smells. Letting the air blow them away just seems so much better. So add a few more hooks on the bottom of the window frame in the bathroom too.

Ironing

There is not much to say about ironing other than it is really boring. Sometimes it is satisfying for about a minute, when you run a really hot iron through some creased cotton and it leaves a line of steaming pressed fabric. But basically, ironing is the horror of all the chores; it is one of those things that piles up higher and higher the longer you leave it. And, of course, the higher the pile gets, the less you want to do it, and once you have done it, it just immediately starts piling up again. The first cheery thing to do with your ironing board is to get a colorful ironing board cover, as it adds the sort of prettiness to the laundry closet that I am talking about. Even if someone else does your ironing this is important because it will make their chore better too.

My one strong recommendation for this job is a lot of steam. It is so easy to chuck starch all over everything as it makes it all so easy to iron, but it also makes your clothes really hard. Starch does have its place; for example, a heavily starched tablecloth is quite glorious and there is that very old-fashioned sight of a Hattie Jacques–style matron in her starched apron and funny hat and, of course, starched ruffled collars. But that, quite frankly, is *it*. I only ever want softness next to my skin—soft, floppy linen and cotton—so steam, girls, and remember to iron in your nightie or panties and bra; it is a hot business. Listen to the radio (a talk radio station is good), and the time soon goes by. Strangely it is a very good time for reflection. I do quite a lot of proper thinking while I am doing the ironing. Sadly, watching a film is not good at all as you can't look up very much.

I would also suggest using a spray can rather than the steamer part of your iron, which is so temperamental.

THE FIRST CHEERY THING TO DO WITH YOUR IRONING BOARD IS TO GET A COLORFUL IRONING BOARD COVER, AS IT ADDS THE SORT OF PRETTINESS TO THE LAUNDRY CLOSET THAT I AM TALKING ABOUT.

You never know when it is going to splat that horrid black stuff all over your clothes. I find it only happens in two instances, the first, of course, being on my brand-new favorite thing that I have never worn and I am trying to gently steam as it cannot take anything more than fairy's breath or it will shrink. The other time is on a shirt that has taken ages to iron and on the last cuff the iron sprays like an octopus all over it, sending it straight back to the laundry basket. It is much safer to wield a spray gun; just be careful you don't get a repetitive strain injury in your wrist and thumb area. I know it sounds daft but once I got repetitive strain injury packing up my flat from pulling Scotch tape over all the boxes and it is really painful.

Now for this fad for lavender water. I have fallen for it and I love it, but it has all got rather expensive and I have found a better way—put a few drops of Hervé's water (see Laundry, above) in the water sprayer. It lasts much longer and makes your clothes smell delicious. I am not sure that lavender water steam is ever very strong, but it can smell awful, so just be careful to find lavender water that you like before you buy it. It is sometimes better to spoil yourself with the good lavender water rather than sticking to the moderate stuff all of the time.

Always iron your sheets and pillowcases (unless you are of the sending-out-to-the-laundry persuasion—see opposite). My friend Natasha irons her sheets on her bed, which is a genius idea. She suggests making sure they come out of the dryer a little damp, which I always find a rather difficult thing to do, for whenever I try to get that perfect iron-damp they are either wet or crispy dry.

Ironing linen and black crêpe needs careful attention, too, as they will burn easily and go shiny, which is just too depressing not least of all because anything made in either of these fabrics is usually expensive. Wool crêpe is light enough that you can just steam it rather than having to have an iron go anywhere near it and a handheld steamer is a valuable asset to the utility closet. They are also easy to pack and can be used when you arrive somewhere with a suitcase full of creased clothes. Linen does require a heavy iron, and so there are two ways: either iron it on the reverse side or put a linen kitchen towel on top of whatever you are ironing to protect it. Personally I find ironing on the reverse side a lot easier; I have never really found that enough heat gets through the towel.

SENDING OUT TO THE LAUNDRY

Everyone has their own luxuries that, come what may, they always have, and laundering sheets is mine. In all the times that I have thought of cutting back on things I should not do, sending my sheets to the laundry is something I simply cannot contemplate sacrificing. When I am feeling financially anorexic I do my pillowcases myself; they aren't too difficult. It is important to remember that when things are a bit tight and you need to cut back, you can't cut back on everything. Afford yourself a couple of luxuries.

If you choose to send things to the laundry, keep a list of everything that goes out; they do lose things and it can be a while before you realize it. Keep a little notebook listing things out and checking them back in again. To lose one pillowcase in a set of sheets is a nightmare, and you need to spot it as soon as possible. You should also be careful of getting the same sheets back as it is not unheard of to be sent somebody else's sheets instead of your own.

Old-fashioned households used to have their names or initials stitched on one of the corners, and not very long ago the laundry used to have those iron-on labels

To lose one pillowcase in a set of sheets is a nightmare, and you need to spot it as soon as possible.

for each customer with their number on it so that items did not go astray. If you are buying sheets from an established company, it is usually possible to have an initial stitched somewhere on them. I did this once for a client because all his sheets and towels were the same and I wanted to make it easy for them to be kept in sets so that they all wore at the same time. Because of the regularity with which sheets get washed, you want to make sure you don't end up with a bed where some of the pillowcases are more washed out than others, and if you are in a position where you have a lot of rooms and someone who looks after your linen and changes your beds, it is much easier for them to find all the things that go together if they are numbered.

Watch out for the sheets being scorched; even the best laundries are quite rough. I have seen beautiful pillowcases with broderie anglaise come back in shreds and you have very little recourse and they are impossible to replace, so whatever happens you have lost out. It is remarkable what little understanding even the best launderers have of what they are dealing with. Sets of bed linen are always surprisingly expensive and you will have trouble getting the value out of the laundry to replace them, so do not send out delicate pillowcases—do them at home—and as soon as you see any sign of scorching happening on your sheets, bring it up and start looking for a new service.

I am quite precious when it comes to the softness of my sheets next to my skin. I have never gone in for silk or satin; in fact I have always found the idea rather slimy and unappealing in bed. You may find that your laundry puts a little starch on the sheets when they are ironing and it is worth requesting that they don't as it makes the sheets hard. This can also result from ironing the sheets with a very hot ironing machine from wet.

DRY CLEANING

Dry cleaning is basically a whole load of rather unpleasant chemicals being thrown at your very best clothes. This is why it is really not always the best thing to do. If you have any clothes with metallic or glamorous buttons make sure you cover them in aluminum foil before they go off to be put through this chemical abuse. Leather can be a problem to dry clean and metallic leather particularly, as can any garment with things glued on, like sequins.

Look at the care label and if there is a P on it, which stands for percloyolethene, then regular dry cleaning should be fine. If there isn't one or even a P with a cross through it, you need to find a specialist dry cleaner who does not use this process. It is really worth checking because, as I said before about laundries, dry cleaners are absolute sharks and will not take responsibility for very much. You see, the label might not have the crossed-out P on it in which case they will argue that they were not warned against the standard practice. It is also monstrously satisfying to have a little inside knowledge when dealing with people that assume you know nothing, rather like car mechanics.

BEDROOMS

I am afraid I don't know what a hospital corner looks like. People have gone on about them for years and I have asked a couple of times but have never really understood their descriptions. I have also not really wanted to know because people give such a derisory look when you don't know, that it instantly makes me think that the whole business of beds and how nurses make them is silly and not something I need to know about.

That said, I do get quite obsessive about my bed and how it is made. I have been known to remake my bed in the middle of the night because the sheets didn't match, and I know that I shouldn't tell stories like that because it only makes me sound ridiculous and thoroughly spoiled and ungrateful that someone else had actually made the bed for me. I also went to boarding school where for a while I had sheets and blankets, despite the general fashion for a duvet, and I got only one clean sheet a week because "they" reckoned somewhere in the dust that was the backs of their heads that the bottom sheet didn't get as dirty as the top sheet. How weird is that? So you gave in one and moved the other; most unsatisfactory, like all school things. One of the things I looked forward to most about coming home was getting into my bed, with delicious soft cotton sheets and lots of squishy fabulous pillows fluffing around my ears. I have never lost that joyous feeling of getting into a beautifully made bed, with heavy blankets on top. In times of trouble and stress, our bed is the place where we seek refuge. It sends us to sleep at the end of a long day and our pillows are what we sob into when things go wrong, so it must really be luxurious to be at all comforting—and of course, more importantly, it has got to be really lovely for the good times too.

When you are making your bed, stretch the sheets as tightly as possible across the mattress, as finding wrinkles is not great. When I get to the corners I fold the sheets like I fold the corners of a present; if you are looking at the end of your mattress with the sheets hanging over the edge, push the left side inward, so you are left with the end of the sheet hanging straight and then lift the corner of the mattress and fold it under as flat as possible. And then do the same with the right side This is important, especially when you have a lot of blankets, because it is no good sleeping with your feet four inches higher than your head. It is important to keep your pillowcases smelling good, especially for guests, so keep some linen spray (or scent if there is no linen spray available) by the bed.

KITCHENS AND BATHROOMS

The kitchen and bathroom are really easy to look after. For me they are the least and most important rooms respectively. I don't spend an awful lot of time in the kitchen, but I do find it an easy room to tidy up because you generally just have to clean, which I quite like. The oven needs attention, and when you clean it be sure to rinse it properly. I fell foul of this when I scrubbed it with a fabulous cleaning spray until it was gleaming clean. But sadly this was not appreciated by my friend Toby, who still maintains that I was trying to poison him when later in the day I cooked roast chicken for him and a few other more polite friends. Don't overlook the fridge either; it gets gross very quickly, so look out for those wipes for the inside of the fridge and microwave, which really do work.

The bathroom is where I like to end a morning's cleaning, where I scrub the whole place down, making sure all the windows are open. Again there are some "once a month" jobs here, too, like taking all your bath and body products off the shelves and cleaning around the lids where they get gloopy and putting them back onto shiny shelves;

scrubbing between the tiles and pouring limescale gel behind the bath plug. This gets really disgusting and it is hard to get to. So pour the gel liberally and wait. It is a good idea to have an old toothbrush handy for those difficult-to-reach cracks and then you just have to rinse and scrub a bit with the toothbrush and the grime runs away down the drain. The trick is definitely in the products (elbow grease is certainly not a product that I like to use on a regular basis).

Once the bathroom is really clean, run a bath, which should signify the end of the morning's hard labor and time to get ready for lunch. There are two very good reasons to save your ablutions until now, the first being that you will need one at this point and the second being that the bathroom will need one too. All those great cleaning products smell disgusting, so if you run a bath filled with delicious oils you will get the place back to smelling like it ought to.

Cleaning glasses

The only route to sparkling glass . . . is a stack of very soft dry cotton or linen cloths. You can only really get glass to sparkle this way, for once a cloth is damp you will never get anything dry with it. Of course, washing by hand is a major bore and I would be lying if I said that that's what always I do. They do go in the dishwasher but more often than not I find I have to dry them when they come out or they get a watermark around the rim. Dishwashers are really not at all good for glass or crystal and eventually they can make them feel squeaky when you touch them, which is a really horrible sensation. The other problem is cloudiness, and to my knowledge neither problem has a cure. So, fill a sink with hot soapy water and add a little vinegar, and then polish your glasses dry with a soft cloth; it will soon get them gleaming. Be careful of very hot water and even more careful of mixing the temperatures. If you are washing a piece of glass with hot water and then change the temperature to very cold it will crack; it is the glass version of a heart attack, I suppose.

Sparkling glass is ravishingly pretty; dull, smeared glass does absolutely nothing for the eye. This is why, if you have enough glasses and aren't too horrified by the prospect of doing the dishes, it is always so much nicer to leave your glasses on the table after dinner and be given new ones when you go back into the sitting room to chat.

Cleaning decanters

Decanters and other similarly shaped bottles can be extremely tiresome to clean, just because it is so frustrating trying to cajole something out of the bottom of a bottle that you can't properly get into. Some necks are so narrow that even a bottlebrush is too big and once in does not really get around the edges satisfactorily. Sand is what you need, or very coarse salt, although the problem with salt is

IF YOU ARE WASHING A PIECE OF GLASS WITH HOT WATER AND THEN CHANGE THE TEMPERATURE TO VERY COLD IT WILL CRACK; IT IS THE GLASS VERSION OF A HEART ATTACK, I SUPPOSE.

that in hot water it will eventually dissolve. So put some sand in the bottom with hot water and dishwashing liquid and start swilling it around. It will loosen any sediment and pour out quite easily.

The next problem is drying the damn things. Of course, where you had a problem in the beginning with the bottle brush, you will now have it with the dish cloth. When I first started buying antiques, my father taught me to dry decanters: rinse with warm water and then move the bottle around and around to create a whirlpool effect inside and with a clever flick of your wrist (practice this with a plastic bottle first), turn it upside down and the whirlpool will rinse the water out so the inside is left almost dry. Following this, dry the outside and then roll up some paper towel on the diagonal to make a long tube (remembering to make it longer than the bottle) and leave it in the bottle overnight. As we are reminded every time we turn on the television, this extremely absorbent towel will remove the last traces of moisture. If you put a stopper in while there is still any water inside, you will get condensation around the neck and if that then dries it will stain and be almost impossible to remove.

Cleaning pans

I love steel wool; it is to pots and pans what a loofah is to the skin. For stoves it removes burned meals with one easy glide of the hand and a little help from that same oven cleaner. You can buy different softnesses at most hardware stores on a roll (contractors use it the whole time), but it is also available with soap: the Brillo pad, made stylish by Andy Warhol. Taking that buildup of burned food off casserole dishes and saucepans gives one such pleasure; it is up there with cleaning silver. When you are rubbing your poor fingers raw with the backside of a sponge it is pure misery, so go for the steel wool. You may have to don rubber gloves, as the feeling of steel wool on the skin bears no resemblance to that of a loofah and is more reminiscent of nails down a blackboard.

Cleaning silver

This is one of the most satisfying of jobs. I don't go in for any of those silver cleaning mitts; they don't really work and take far too much rubbing if they are going to work at all. Instead, go for the cream that comes in a tub with a sponge and then rinse with warm water; you really do need to get rid of all the cream. If the piece of silver you are cleaning has any intricate engraving or ridges, you may need to use a soft brush to remove the silver polish from these areas. A soft toothbrush usually does the trick very successfully. I find it quite unappealing when you see beautiful candlesticks that still have silver polish caked in the difficult-to-get-to areas. Dry thoroughly and you will have a delight for the eye.

Don't put anything abrasive near silver as it is a very soft metal and you will scratch it. I did this once and it is expensive to rectify, although it is possible. Take scratched silver to a silversmith and he will buff it up for you and take out any dents. The only problem with this is that, of course, you wear the silver down a little every time you do it.

POST-DINNER PARTY CLEANUP

Everyone seems to have very clear ideas about when they like to clean up after a dinner party. All I can tell you is that I don't believe there are many things that can make a hangover worse than a stack of dirty dishes that hasn't even made it to the kitchen sink interspersed with full ashtrays and old bottles of wine. So, however late, do it the night before, and if you can't bear all of it, just do some basic damage control. The ideal is to have a friend stay with you while you do this; he or she is not there necessarily to help but to sit, chat and do a general postmortem of the evening with you while you clean up. I know the idea of the friend sitting down while you slave around her or him sounds pretty awful, but you will get it done so much more quickly if you are not a) moving around someone else and b) constantly being asked where things go. Gossiping while you work makes the time fly by.

Once this is done you can go back into the living room, plump up the cushions, which takes precisely no time, and it's done. Sit down and have one last drink with your friend and then off you go to bed. Some of the best conversations you will ever have are after a dinner with the one person who stays behind. The kitchen sink is also a great place for chewing the fat. There is something quite therapeutic about washing and chatting—I promise!

Votive candle holders and candlesticks

It doesn't take many candlelit dinners to positively clog up your finest candlesticks and little glass votive candle holders. Candlesticks can and do look rather marvelous with years of dripped wax down them and I think the fashion for nondrip candles is probably rather over. However, there are times when you really want everything to be sparkling and new again. Basins of piping hot water are all that you need, which will loosen the wax and it will simply drop off. You do need to take care, though, because like hot fat, you must not let it all just run away down the drain or you are going to be left with a clogged pipe. So make sure you leave enough space in the sink to run the cold water to solidify the melted wax, which you can then remove by hand and throw in the trash. You will need to give everything a jolly good wash again with hot water and dishwashing liquid to get rid of the greasy film that will have been left behind after the original soak.

By the way, if you have glass candlesticks you must pay attention to the candle burning down the inside of the

glass holder. Unless the glass is very thick it will break, leaving the candlestick's destiny with the trash. It is the most obvious thing in the world, but usually only with hindsight. Which is how I learned this.

Wax dripping on the table or tablecloth

I think that everyone knows that to get candle wax out of fabric you need to iron it with some brown paper over the top of the wax, but I feel it must be mentioned. Be careful of the newspaper, however, because if the fabric is at all wet you could end up with the day's headlines on your favorite damask cloth, forever immortalizing the day of repair. And use a very low heat.

If you have a wooden dining table and do not want always to use a cloth to protect it or nondrip candles, there are two options open to you. One is the little glass collars that you can get to put around the base of the candle and the other is to use large mirrored coasters. You can find these in antique shops. They were originally made for vases to sit on to protect the furniture and are still ideal for that, but they are particularly pretty with the candlelight reflected in them.

THE HOME DESK

The idea of working at home for many is a horrifying one. If you have an office, the last thing you want to go home to is a pile of papers. But it is important to keep a tidy grip on housekeeping, especially all those household bills and wretched appliance guarantees that you can never find when your dishwasher floods the kitchen. There are two options for this: have all your household bills and bank statements sent to your work so you can tackle them while you are in that frame of mind, or have the files at home.

For bills I find it is important to have a bills file and to pay them all once a month. I used to get so confused by bills, lose them and then find myself about to be cut off from all outside communication simply because the telephone bill was under a pile of rubbish on my desk. As you receive these bills put them in a folder and put them away, and then when you get your paycheck sit down and pay them all at once and file them.

There is something very satisfying about doing it in this way as paying your bills when you are ready gives a satisfying feeling of being in control. Furthermore, the really cool thing is that when you come to sit down and write all the checks, you do it when you know there is money in your account rather than that terrible thing of just praying it will work. You have completed a task, too; moving paper from one pile to another, posting a bunch of envelopes and filing the bills is a job done, which always feels good. Don't pay too much attention to how much money you have just spent.

Clippings files and bulletin boards

Magazines can start taking up a lot of space. Indeed, I have trouble seeing the television screen over my coffee table now for the towers of back issues that have gathered there. The trouble is it is more difficult to throw away a large amount of magazines than it is just to keep them; they are extremely heavy and split the sides of the trash bags. The answer is to throw them out as soon as you have read them. But clip them first as there is often stuff in magazines that is quite inspiring and you might want to refer back to something at some stage. The truth is that you never find it again if it is left in the magazine, because you will never remember which magazine and issue it was in.

Clippings files are very useful for reference and I refer to mine quite often. Divide the file up into sections, so you have color schemes, floors, bookcases, flowers, exterior colors. Even if you think they are things that will never be useful, painting the outside of your house is quite difficult to do when it actually comes down to it and there are so many cool things that you can do other than white, but it is hard to think of them when you have a contractor breathing down your neck. The color section can be anything from a pile of leaves to jars of olive oil.

Bulletin boards are a very important thing to have in the office as they give your work space a little personality and they are good reminders of things. If you get a postcard from a company that you want to be reminded about, don't file it because you will never look at it again. Pin up anything that pleases your eye, and a random work of art will appear after a while. Remember to edit it from time to time; they can become rather a mess and there will be things that bore you after a bit.

DOMESTIC STAFF

Staff are a really tricky subject. Everyone seems to gasp when I mention it but staff at home are really no different from staff in an office except that your home is their office and your vacuum their laptop. So they are entitled to be treated in the same way. I have so many friends who have little to no communication with the lady who cleans their flat or house. Admittedly, if you have a nine-to-five job this can happen really easily, but it is wrong for two reasons. First, can you imagine anything worse than never seeing or communicating with your boss? Second, it means that the domestic angel in question rarely continues to do a good job. It would be unthinkable to employ new staff in your office and show them to their desks on the first day, show them where the kettle and the bathroom are and then never give them any more direction, so the same rules should apply at home.

FURTHERMORE, THE REALLY COOL THING IS THAT WHEN YOU COME TO SIT DOWN AND WRITE ALL THE CHECKS, YOU DO IT WHEN YOU KNOW THERE IS MONEY IN YOUR ACCOUNT RATHER THAN THAT TERRIBLE THING OF JUST PRAYING IT WILL WORK.

The other thing I find weird on the domestic staff front are their job titles. I have been laughed at and teased for calling them maids, and I stopped a while ago as it seems to be too old-fashioned and strange. But I have to say that I would so much rather be a maid than a daily. I now get teased for using the word "daily." I don't actually have one, but my friend Kevin screamed the other day when I talked about my old daily. I apparently sound ridiculously snobby and should call her the help or the cleaner. Well, I mean, I have never heard two sadder job descriptions. Can you imagine having your business cards made up with your name and then "Help" underneath? It is really the most depressing thing to have to say when someone asks you what you do. So give your housekeeper a little dignity and some job satisfaction and direct her in the same way that you would like to be directed in your own job.

Hiring domestic staff

It is quite hard to know what to say to your new, let's call her the domestic angel (that is my favorite job title), on her first day. They are even harder to interview, as nobody is going to say that the way they like to wash your white La Perla is in hot water with your husband's black cashmere socks, are they? That always confuses me, they know it's wrong and yet they still do it. I once interviewed a domestic witch for a client and it was one of the questions that I asked. She looked at me with such disgust for being so impertinent, like who do you think I am, but then the first thing she did was put everything (and I mean everything: beautiful dish towels I had bought in an antique market, Robin's favorite blue and white check shirt, some blue socks and a few pillowcases) in to boil for a few hours. So interviewing is really a waste of time.

Even worse, never trust written references. If you are going to, you must call the previous employers and ask them all sorts of questions. Many people feel embarrassed to hand someone a reference which basically says they were rubbish at their job. They think that as they are not their problem anymore it doesn't matter if they say that they were great, whereas they might be more honest on the telephone. Watch out for references that stress reliable and trustworthy—it does not keep the woodwork clean.

Also remember to employ someone with whom you share a language. It sounds like ridiculous advice but you would be amazed how many people leave their homes in the hands of someone who has no idea what they are talking about.

Directing your newfound staff

You will only get out what you are prepared to put in. The first time the new domestic angel comes to your house, take the morning off work to go over everything. Show her where everything is, give her some money so she can buy the products she likes using and find out if there is anything that she needs. Make sure she has your telephone number at work so she can contact you, and call her from the office if there is anything you would like to go over with her.

So to the instructions. First, leave a list of the things that you want done. There will obviously be all the usual dishwashing, bed making, bathroom cleaning, etc., that don't need mentioning but you will probably need to show her how you like your bed made. Put one extra thing on each time, so one week it will be clean the tops of the windowsills, wash all the woodwork (doors and baseboards get very grubby), the floors, vacuum behind the so-

It would be unthinkable to employ new staff in your office and show them to their desks on the first day, show them where the kettle and the bathroom are and then never give them any more direction, so the same rules should apply at home.

fas. All of those areas are places that get forgotten, and because you are not a trained housekeeper yourself, these aren't the things you naturally think of, until you pull back your sofa to find something and find an inch of dust.

It is not embarrassing to leave someone instructions; you neither have to bark them at her nor apologize for them—just be straightforward. When they are done well, let her know and then you can also let her know when she has done it really badly or not at all. Remember, you don't get away with doing a slack job. When was the last time your boss let you get away with low-grade work, and how much respect would you have for your boss if he or she were too embarrassed to take you to task for it? Well, none, would you? And yet so many people don't do anything about their domestic staff leaving the windowsills to get so dusty that they are black.

With regard to laundry instructions, do not assume anything about your angel's knowledge of wool crêpe care. It can be an enormously expensive and sad assumption that she knows what she is doing. If you are going to leave all your clothes on the floor and expect her to know what to do, then you run the risk of tragedy. It is far better to leave a pile of clothes with notes on each item for what you want doing with them, i.e., hand washing, dry cleaning, pressing or mending.

Human contact is really important. Remember her birthday, and at Christmas you need to give her a bonus, the same as you get in an office. This is traditionally an extra month's salary, but if you can't afford to do it, then a small present is just as nice. I just believe they need to feel that they have a place in the home, that they are your lifesavers.

. . . DO NOT ASSUME ANYTHING ABOUT YOUR ANGEL'S KNOWLEDGE OF WOOL CRÊPE CARE. IT CAN BE AN ENORMOUSLY EXPENSIVE AND SAD ASSUMPTION THAT SHE KNOWS WHAT SHE IS DOING.

ACKNOWLEDGMENTS

A good project can never really be successful without the help and support of an awful lot of people, and this one is no exception. I must thank William Seighart for making that call to Ed Victor, who by some miracle not only agreed to see me, but took me on and put me in the remarkably safe and capable hands of Lizzy Kremer. I cannot recommend great agents highly enough—they take you by the hand, pamper and boost you all the way, and then make you money in the process. It is just fantastic.

I would also like to thank Cindy Richards, who first suggested I do a book. While a collaboration between us never materialized, if she hadn't planted the original seed, a book would never have appeared.

I would like to thank Alexandra Shulman in particular. She created "Rita Says," my column in *Vogue*, because she had a hunch that domestic would be big. Let's hope so! Thank you for taking me on and setting me on my way.

Denise Bates at Ebury Press took the carrot. Thank you so much—I am so thrilled that we have done this book together. It seems to have been a total breeze, which I know it is not supposed to be, rock on the next one.

I owe a huge thank-you to Trish Todd and Doris Cooper for taking *Domestic Bliss* to America. I hope that we will have a wonderful success with it. And a little extra thank-you to Doris for being so unbelievably patient with me and being so cautious and sympathetic with the various changes. I must thank London King for all her tremendous help with the press and marketing of the book and all at Fireside for their support and enthusiasm.

Thank you Caz Hildebrand for making this book look so pretty and not verbalizing how insane I must have driven you when I wanted to see every illustrator's book on the planet before making a choice, even though you had already spotted Sam Wilson, who has brought *Domestic Bliss* alive with her beautiful illustrations.

The sales force cannot possibly go without a big fat thank-you. They are a band of merry men and women who travel around the country selling this book, without whom *Domestic Bliss* would never see a bookshelf—thank you.

In particular I must thank Colin and Isabella Cawdor and Eck and Lucy Ogilvie-Grant, my great, great friends who stowed me away in the Highlands during the last critical "get on with it" month of writing.

And lastly I would like to mention Glen Luchford, whose support, wisdom and advice helped change the path of my career and directly influenced the direction that this book has taken. It is to you, Glen, that I dedicate *Domestic Bliss*, with lots of love and heartfelt thanks.

Contributing friends who helped more than they can possibly know:

Nina Campbell
Thank you for sitting up late one night to go through the American edit and for bringing the curry with you too!

Matt Darby
An avid camper who drove my friend Gina and me on our

first camping trip when the camper van company, probably sensibly, refused to insure either of us to drive it. He helped me enormously with the camping section—thank you.

Honor Fraser

Thank you for your pearls of domestic wisdom. They are always brilliant and certainly never run-of-the-mill, which of course would be unlikely from you.

Helen and George Gardiner

Thank you for teaching me so much about antiques and about buying them, for taking me to my first flea market in a field and for becoming such friends. I wish that George were still around to read my book, even though I know that he would say it was a load of frivolous nonsense!

Natasha Garnett

You will see yourself quite a bit in the book. Thank you for your ideas, for our party that we dreamed up on a boring old January day—it inspired so many brilliant things—and for your advice.

Robin Houldsworth

Robin employed me on my first decorating job. Thank you—it taught me a lot, and gave me a lot of material for this book. I am sure that you will recognize a few bits!

Jane Leaver

Jane is my fairy godmother, and she was my Jewish adviser for this book when I was trying to find out if giving honey was a Jewish custom. It took some nagging, as she insisted that really champagne is almost always a preferred gift, Jewish or not.

David Linley

Thank you for being such a mate, for your advice when I needed it and the help you offered with the text.

Jo Malone

Jo has been a friend for a long time and was so generous with her knowledge while I was writing about scenting the home. Thank goodness, because I can't think of another person I could have asked and whose opinion I would have trusted.

JJ O'Brien

You know what you did, it was amazing and I can't ever thank you enough.

Lucy Ogilvy-Grant

It just isn't enough to thank you with Eck for having me to stay—you have been such an inspiration to me. You appear a lot throughout this book—I hope you like it.

Phil Poynter

Thank you for demanding to read the first draft—you were the first friend to read *Domestic Bliss* and I was more nervous of what you thought than of any of the big cheeses. Thank you for saying such lovely things; I can't think that it was an easy task wading through all that loose paper.

Rowan Somerville

You get a big thank-you—you are scattered throughout this book. Thank you for the real-life domestic bliss we enjoyed, despite there always being a lot of flat-leaf parsley on the kitchen floor.

Willy Stirling

A star within the home renovations section, as well as making a few guest appearances in the camping section. Thank you for helping me with the main body of "Dealing with Contractors."

I would like to thank the following people for their help with various sections and for taking the time to share their tips:

Nicole Bellamy, Laura Campbell, Dave Cazelet, Alice Deen, Catri Drummond, Sarita Gainza, Annabel Giles, Fiona Golfar, Magnus Goodlad, Charlie Hardy, Gavin Houghton, Tessa Kennedy, Elly Klein, Willy Klein, Kevin Kollenda, Max Konig, Dan Lywood, Edna O'Brien, Sarah O'Keefe, Gillian McVey, Nigel Peters, Gawain Rainey, Piers Thompson and William Yeoward.

INDEX

THE AUTHOR

RITA KONIG began her career as a researcher for *Harpers & Queen*, *Mirabella* and *Town and Country* before working as a buyer for Nina Campbell Interiors. Rita now works as a decorator for a range of clients, both commercial and private. Rita has a column in the Saturday *Telegraph* and since 2000 has written the cult column in *Vogue*, "Rita Says." *Domestic Bliss* is her first book.